3D Origami Platonic Solids & More

Other books by John Montroll
www.johnmontroll.com

General Origami

Origami Worldwide
Teach Yourself Origami: Second Revised Edition
Christmas Origami
Storytime Origami
Origami Inside-Out: Second Revised Edition

Animal Origami

Dragons and Other Fantastic Creatures in Origami
Bugs in Origami
Horses in Origami
Origami Birds
Origami Gone Wild
Dinosaur Origami
Origami Dinosaurs for Beginners
Mythological Creatures and the Chinese Zodiac Origami
Origami Under the Sea
Sea Creatures in Origami
Origami Sea Life
Bringing Origami to Life
Bugs and Birds in Origami
Origami Sculptures
African Animals in Origami: Second Revised Edition
North American Animals in Origami: Second Revised Edition

Geometric Origami

Origami Stars
Galaxy of Origami Stars
Origami and Math: Simple to Complex
Origami & Geometry
3D Origami Diamonds
3D Origami Antidiamonds
Classic Polyhedra Origami
A Constellation of Origami Polyhedra
A Plethora of Polyhedra in Origami
Origami Polyhedra Design

Dollar Bill Origami

Dollar Origami Treasures
Dollar Bill Animals in Origami
Dollar Bill Origami
Easy Dollar Bill Origami

Simple Origami

Fun and Simple Origami: 101 Easy-to-Fold Projects
Super Simple Origami
Easy Dollar Bill Origami
Easy Origami Animals
Origami Twelve Days of Christmas: And Santa, Too!

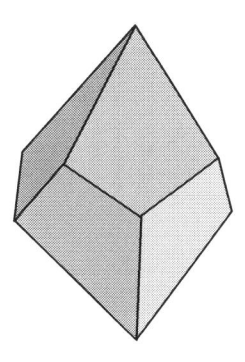

3D Origami Platonic Solids & More

Each from a single square!

John Montroll

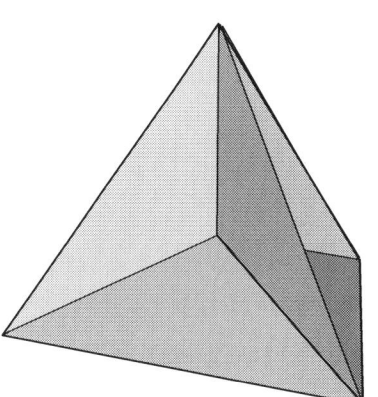

Antroll Publishing Company

3D Origami Platonic Solids & More

Copyright © 2012 by John Montroll. All rights reserved.
No part of this publication may be copied or reproduced by any
means without the express written permission of the author.

ISBN-10: 1480217514
ISBN-13: 978-1480217515

Antroll Publishing Company

Introduction

Polyhedra are incredibly beautiful shapes. Here is a collection of around 30 models including the five Platonic Solids, sunken versions of each, models with color patterns, variations on Archimedean Solids, and more.

The folding methods for each of these interesting models are amazingly different. All are original designs, using the latest in folding techniques. Each model is folded from a single square, which makes them more amazing and satisfying. They range from simple to complex.

The folding techniques combine the art of origami with geometry. Many of the models were designed using math so as to fold them as simply as possible. There is information on symmetry, which is used to understand and simplify the folding patterns. Included are sections on Octahedra and Dodecahedra, polyhedra with eight and twelve sides. This adds variety to families of shapes including a prism, antiprism, dipyramid, and trapezohedron.

The illustrations conform to the internationally accepted Randlett-Yoshizawa conventions. You can use any kind of square paper for these models, but the best results can be achieved using standard origami paper, which is colored on one side and white on the other. In these diagrams, the shading represents the colored side. Origami paper can be found in many hobby shops or on several online sites including www.origami-usa.org.

I am a pioneer in designing origami polyhedra from a single sheet. Through origami ideas combined with math, I have been able to create a long list of polyhedra which is not so difficult to fold. Related books on this subject include *Classic Polyhedra Origami*. I hope this collection inspires you to continue with this topic.

John Montroll
www.johnmontroll.com

Symbols 8
Basic Folds 9
Symmetry 10
Platonic Solids 11
Sunken Platonic Solids 31
Inside-Out Platonic Solids 50
Dimpled Polyhedra 69
Octahedra 86
Dodecahedra 100

Contents

★ Simple
★★ Intermediate
★★★ Complex
★★★★ Very Complex

Platonic Solids

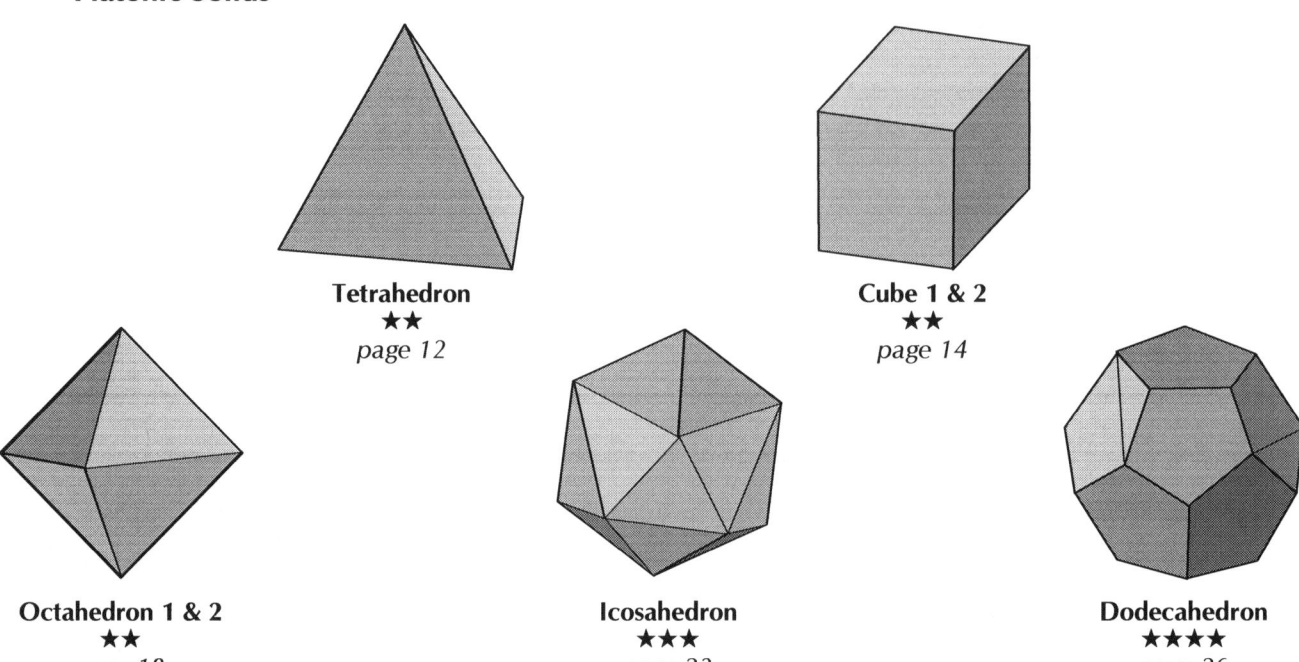

Tetrahedron
★★
page 12

Cube 1 & 2
★★
page 14

Octahedron 1 & 2
★★
page 18

Icosahedron
★★★
page 23

Dodecahedron
★★★★
page 26

Sunken Platonic Solids

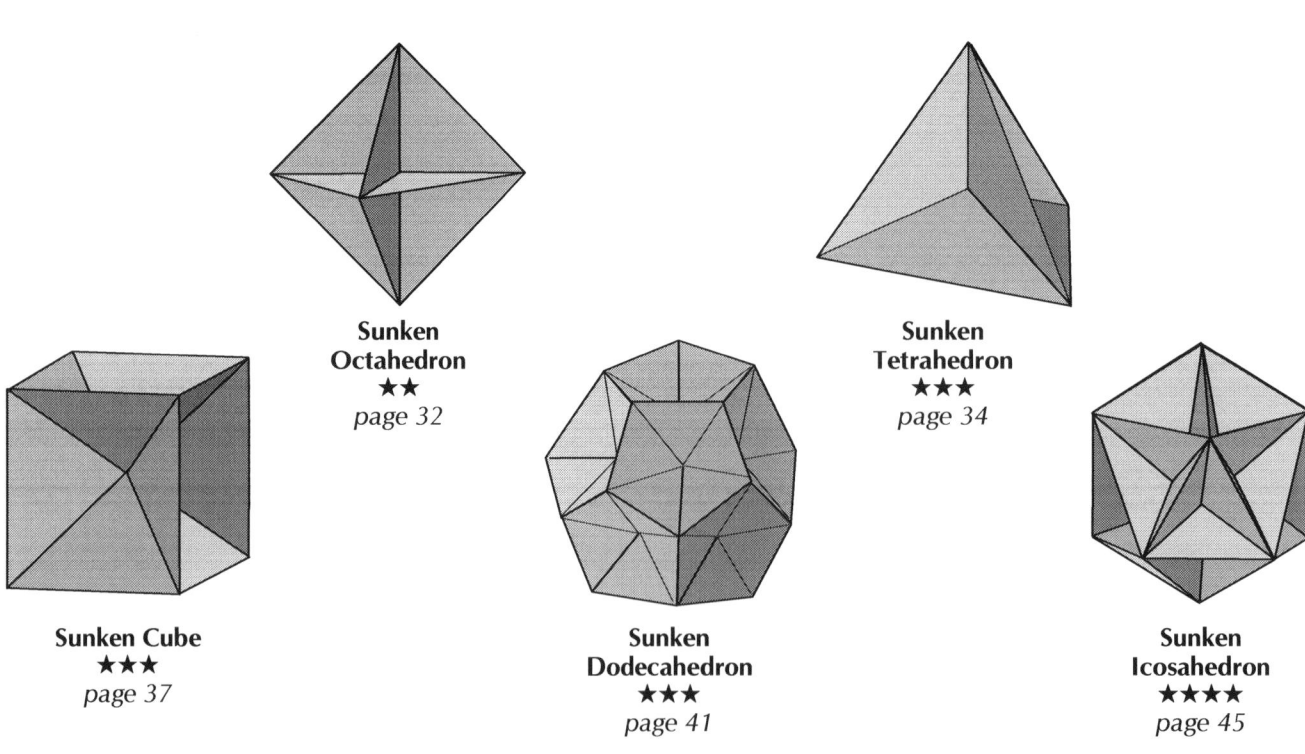

Sunken Octahedron
★★
page 32

Sunken Tetrahedron
★★★
page 34

Sunken Cube
★★★
page 37

Sunken Dodecahedron
★★★
page 41

Sunken Icosahedron
★★★★
page 45

6 *3D Origami Platonic Solids & More*

Inside-Out Platonic Solids

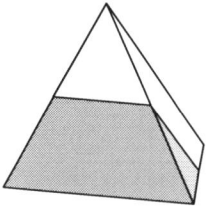
Duo-Striped Tetrahedron
★★
page 51

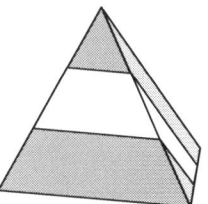
Layered Tetrahedron
★★
page 54

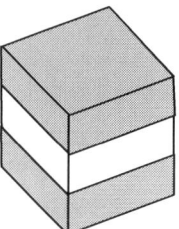
Three-Layered Cube
★★
page 57

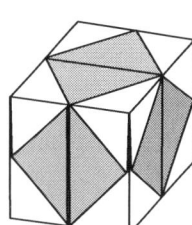
Fancy Cube
★★
page 60

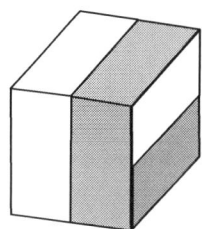
Banded Cube
★★
page 63

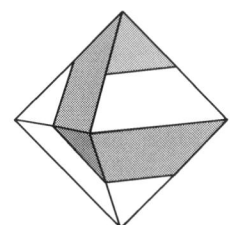
Banded Octahedron
★★
page 66

Dimpled Polyhedra

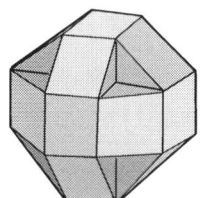
Dimpled Rhombicuboctahedron
★★★
page 69

Cubehemioctahedron
★★★
page 73

Octahemioctahedron
★★★
page 77

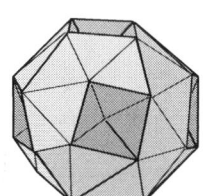
Dimpled Snub Cube
★★★
page 81

Octahedra

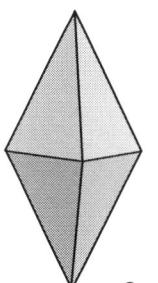
Square Dipyramid
★★
page 87

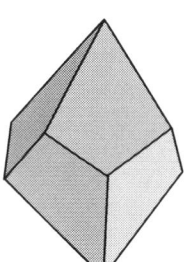
Square Trapezohedron
★★★
page 89

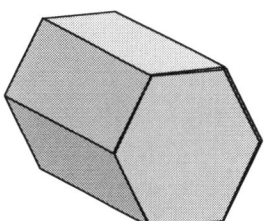
Hexagonal Prism
★★★
page 93

Triangular Antiprism
★★★
page 97

Dodecahedra

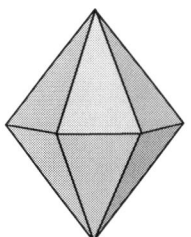
Hexagonal Dipyramid
★★★
page 101

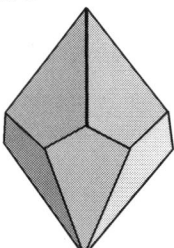
Hexagonal Trapezohedron
★★★
page 104

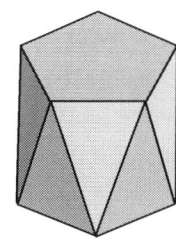
Golden Pentagonal Antiprism
★★★
page 108

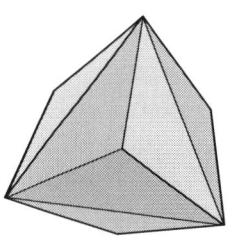
Triakis Tetrahedron
★★★
page 112

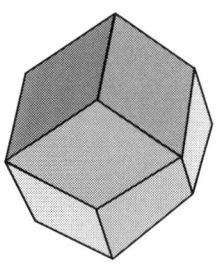
Rhombic Dodecahedron
★★★
page 116

Symbols

Lines

——————— Valley fold, fold in front.

—··—··—··—··— Mountain fold, fold behind.

—————————— Crease line.

·················· X-ray or guide line.

Arrows

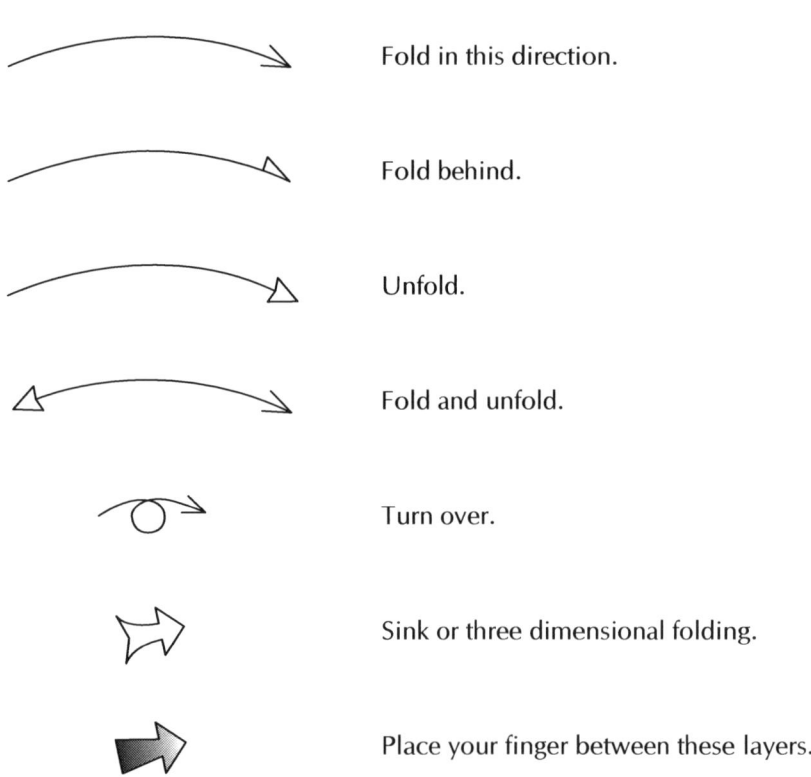

Fold in this direction.

Fold behind.

Unfold.

Fold and unfold.

Turn over.

Sink or three dimensional folding.

Place your finger between these layers.

Basic Folds

Squash Fold.

In a squash fold, some paper is opened and then made flat. The shaded arrow shows where to place your finger.

1
Squash-fold.

2
A 3D step.

3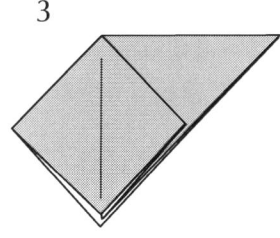

Inside Reverse Fold.

In an inside reverse fold, some paper is folded between layers. Here are two examples.

1
Reverse-fold.

2

1
Reverse-fold.

2

Preliminary Fold.

The Preliminary Fold is the starting point for many models. The maneuver in step 3 occurs in many other models.

1
Fold and unfold.

2
Fold and unfold.

3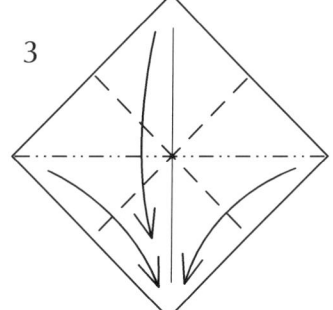
Collapse the square by bringing the four corners together.

4
This is 3D.

5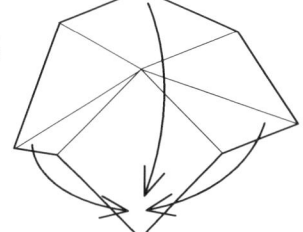
Preliminary Fold

Basic Folds

Symmetry

Each model in this collection is folded from a square sheet of paper. To design these complex three-dimensional shapes, I want to satisfy several conditions that include:
1. The model is not too difficult to fold.
2. The paper is used efficiently to produce a shape as large as possible.
3. The model holds together well.
4. Each face has no stray lines, or a minimal number.
5. The folding procedure is as simple as possible, with fewest number of steps.

Symmetry simplifies the folding procedure. Symmetry can be seen by looking at the crease pattern of a model. The crease pattern shows the unfolded square sheet where the shaded regions represent the faces of the model, and the orientation of these regions shows the form of symmetry.

Five forms of symmetry are used in this work, and the five Platonic solids can be folded which use each of them. Here are the forms of symmetry.

Even Symmetry: Two sides of the square are mirror images. The tetrahedron uses even symmetry.

Tetrahedron

Odd Symmetry: The crease pattern is the same when rotated 180°. The icosahedron uses odd symmetry.

Icosahedron

Square Symmetry: The crease pattern is the same when rotated 90°. The octahedron uses square symmetry.

Octahedron

3/4 Square Symmetry: The crease pattern is the same when rotated 90°, but one of four quadrants is not used. The cube uses 3/4 square symmetry.

Cube

No Symmetry: The crease pattern shows no symmetry. The dodecahedron has no symmetry.

Dodecahedron

10   *3D Origami Platonic Solids & More*

Platonic Solids

The five Platonic solids are the tetrahedron, cube, octahedron, icosahedron, and dodecahedron. They are the only polyhedra with the following properties:

1. The faces of each are identical regular polygons.

2. The corners of each are alike.

3. The shapes are convex. For convex polyhedra, line segments connecting any two corners are on or inside the solid.

To Plato, the tetrahedron represented fire, the cube represented earth, the octahedron represented air, the icosahedron represented water, and the dodecahedron represented the universe.

Here are the five Platonic solids with number of faces for each.

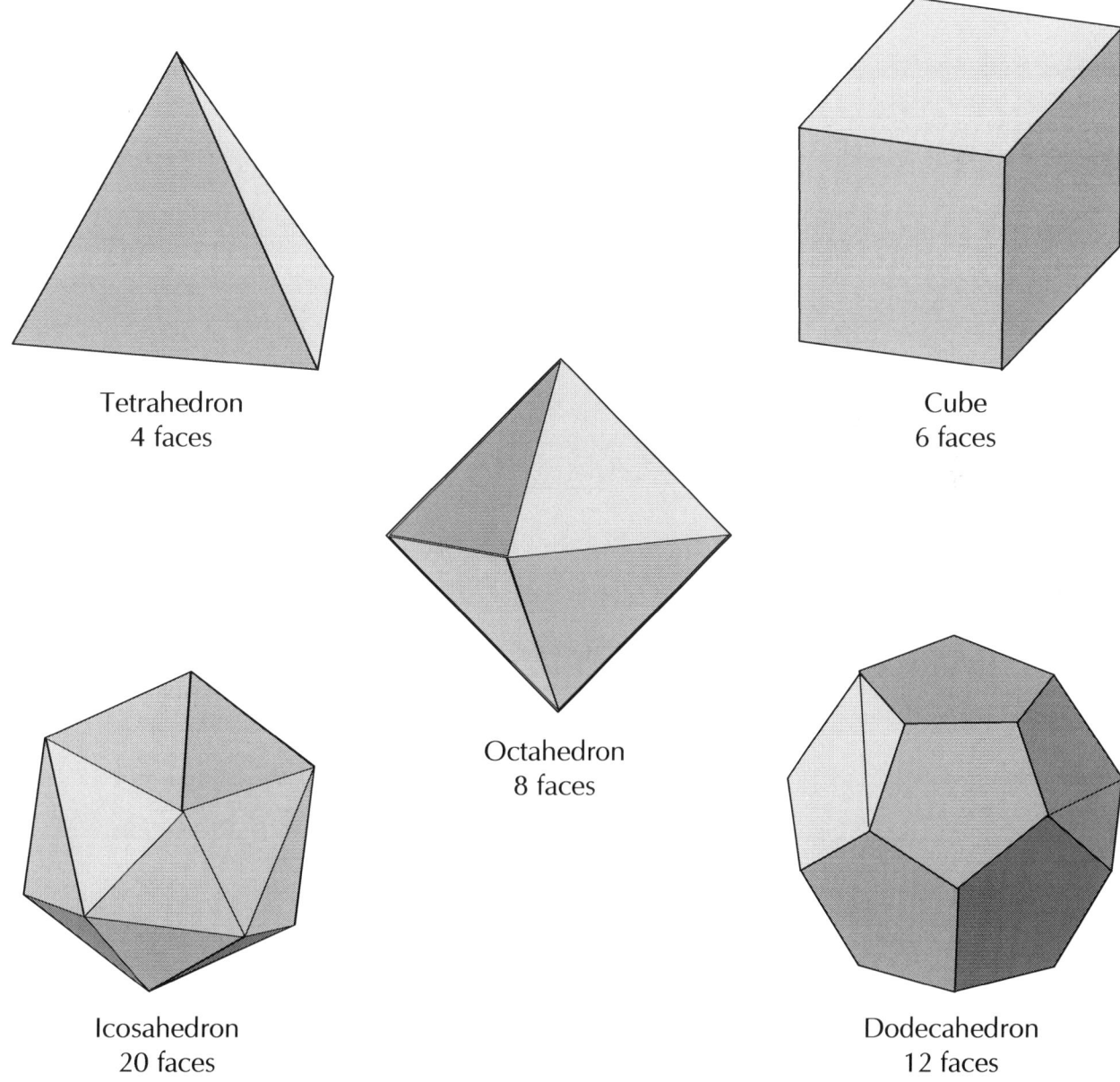

Tetrahedron
4 faces

Cube
6 faces

Octahedron
8 faces

Icosahedron
20 faces

Dodecahedron
12 faces

Tetrahedron

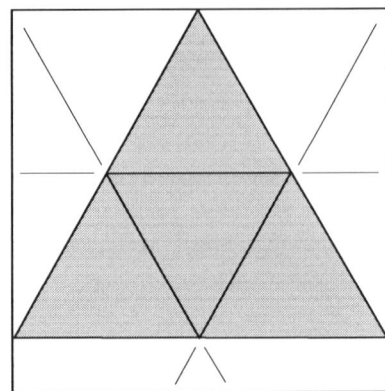

Composed of four equilateral triangles, this is the simplest of the five Platonic solids. Plato believed the tetrahedron represented fire because of its sharpness and simplicity.

The figure above shows the crease pattern. Even symmetry is used.

1

Fold and unfold on the left and right.

2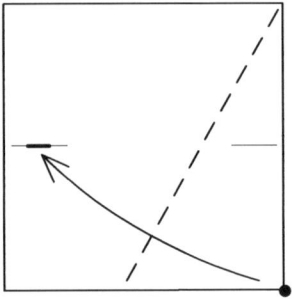

Bring the lower right corner to the line.

3

Unfold.

4

Fold and unfold.

5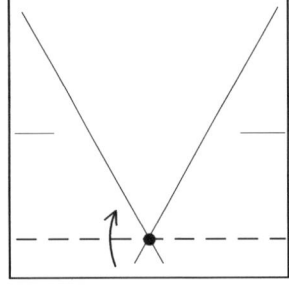

Fold up at the intersection.

6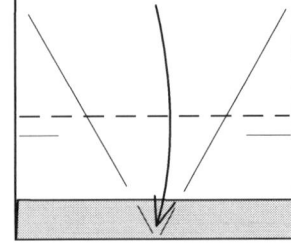

12   *3D Origami Platonic Solids & More*

7

Unfold.

8

9

10

Unfold.

11

Fold and unfold at 45°.

12

Fold along the creases.

13

Reverse folds.

14

Lift up at the dot in the center. The other two dots will meet and the model will become 3D.

15

tab

Tuck the tab inside. The dots will meet.

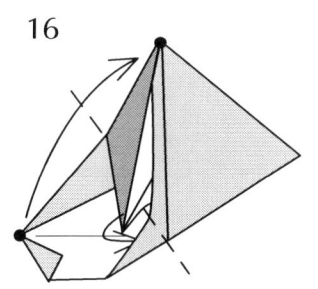

16

Cover the dark triangle.

17

Tuck inside.

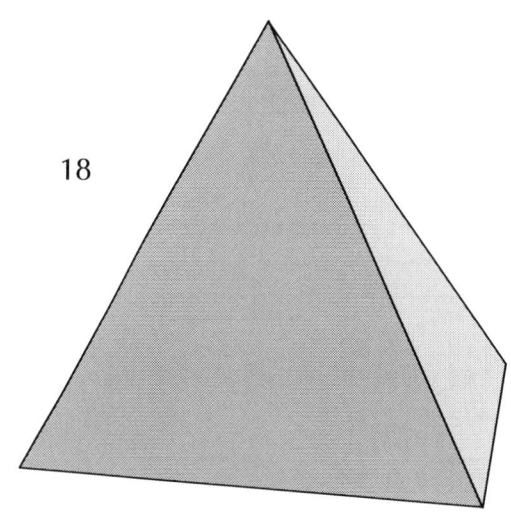

18

Tetrahedron

Cube (1)

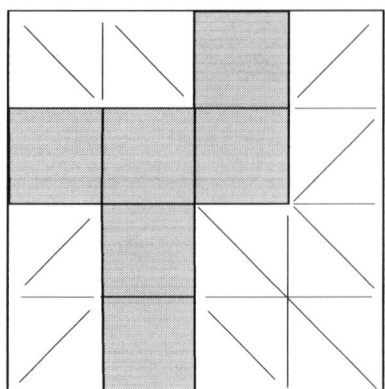

Plato believed the cube, with six square faces, symbolized earth because of its stability.

This model uses 3/4 square symmetry and is slightly easier to fold than the next cube.

1

Fold and unfold.

2

Fold and unfold.

3

Fold and unfold.

4

Fold and unfold.

5

Fold and unfold.

6
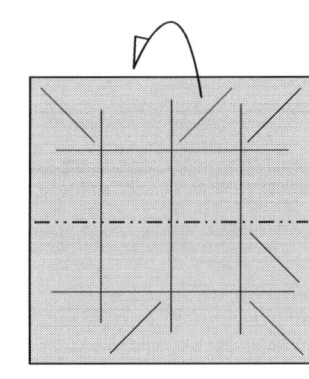

14   *3D Origami Platonic Solids & More*

Cube 15

Cube (2)

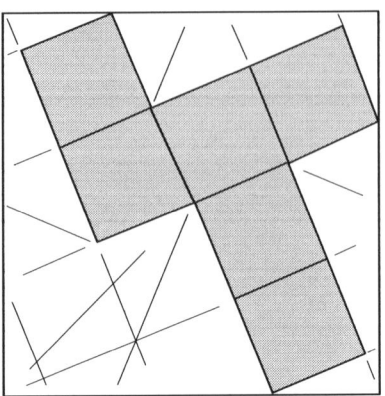

This folding method produces a larger cube than the previous model. However, there is less tab to lock the cube. The crease pattern shows 3/4 square symmetry.

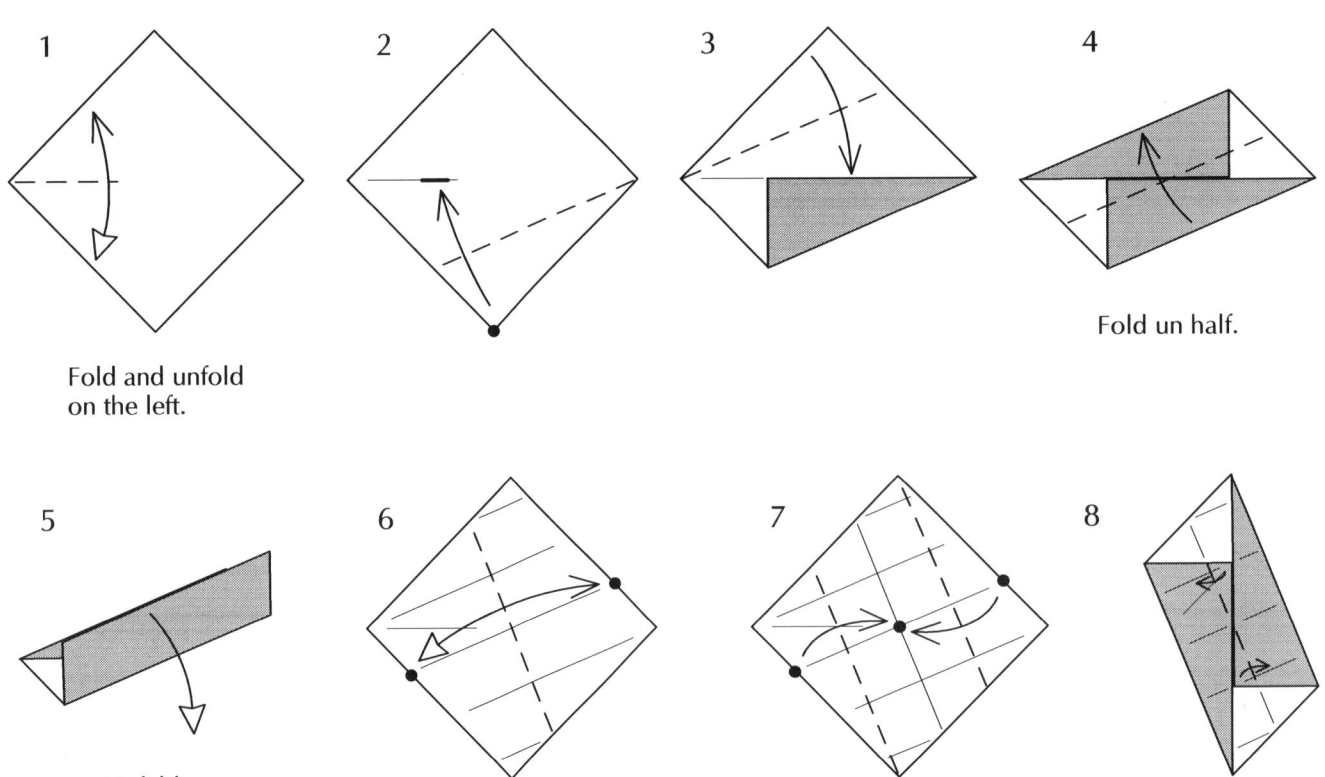

1. Fold and unfold on the left.
2.
3.
4. Fold un half.
5. Unfold.
6. Fold and unfold.
7.
8. Fold along a partially hidden crease.

16 *3D Origami Platonic Solids & More*

9

Unfold.

10

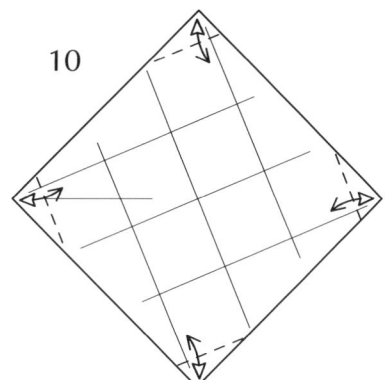

Fold and unfold along the creases.

11

Fold and unfold. Rotate 90°.

12

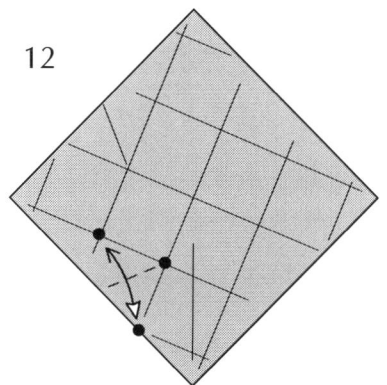

Repeat step 11 three more times.

13

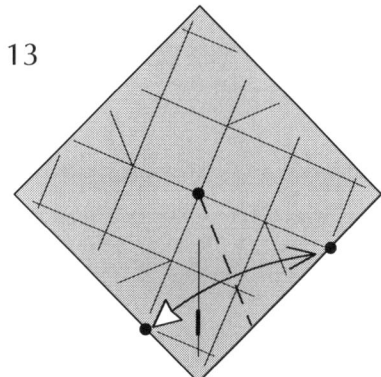

Note the orientation of the vertical crease by the bottom. Fold and unfold.

14

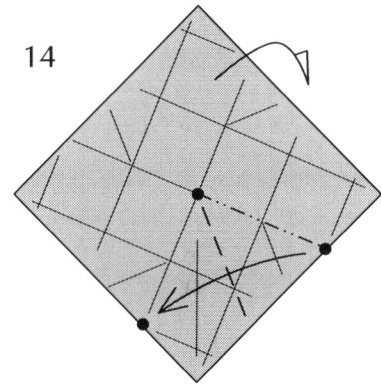

Puff out at the dot in the center as the model becomes 3D.

15

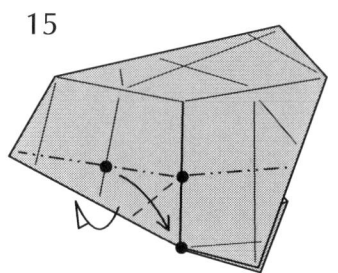

Puff out at the dot in the center and flatten inside.

16

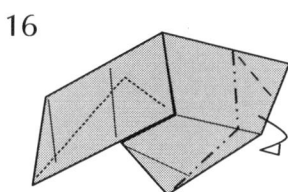

Flatten the inside paper shown with the x-ray lines. Repeat step 15 two more times. Rotate the loose corners to the top. One side has more layers.

17

Fold and unfold. Repeat on the other two flaps.

18

Interlock the three tabs to close and lock the model.

19

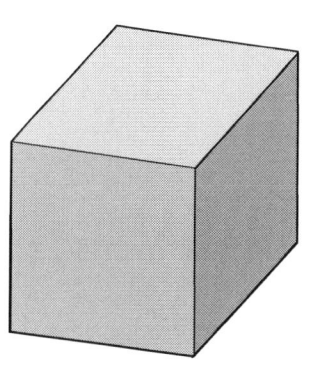

Cube

Cube 17

Octahedron (1)

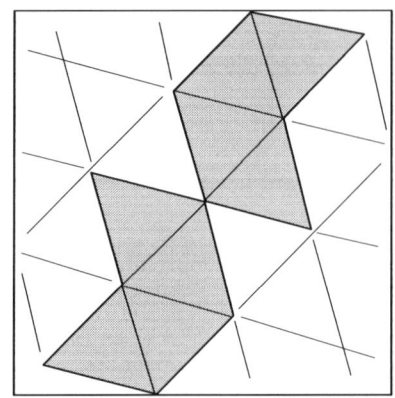

The octahedron, formed from eight equilateral triangles, represented air to Plato because it appears to be suspended.

This version is easier to fold than the next. The folding method is 2D until the last step when it is inflated. Odd symmetry is used.

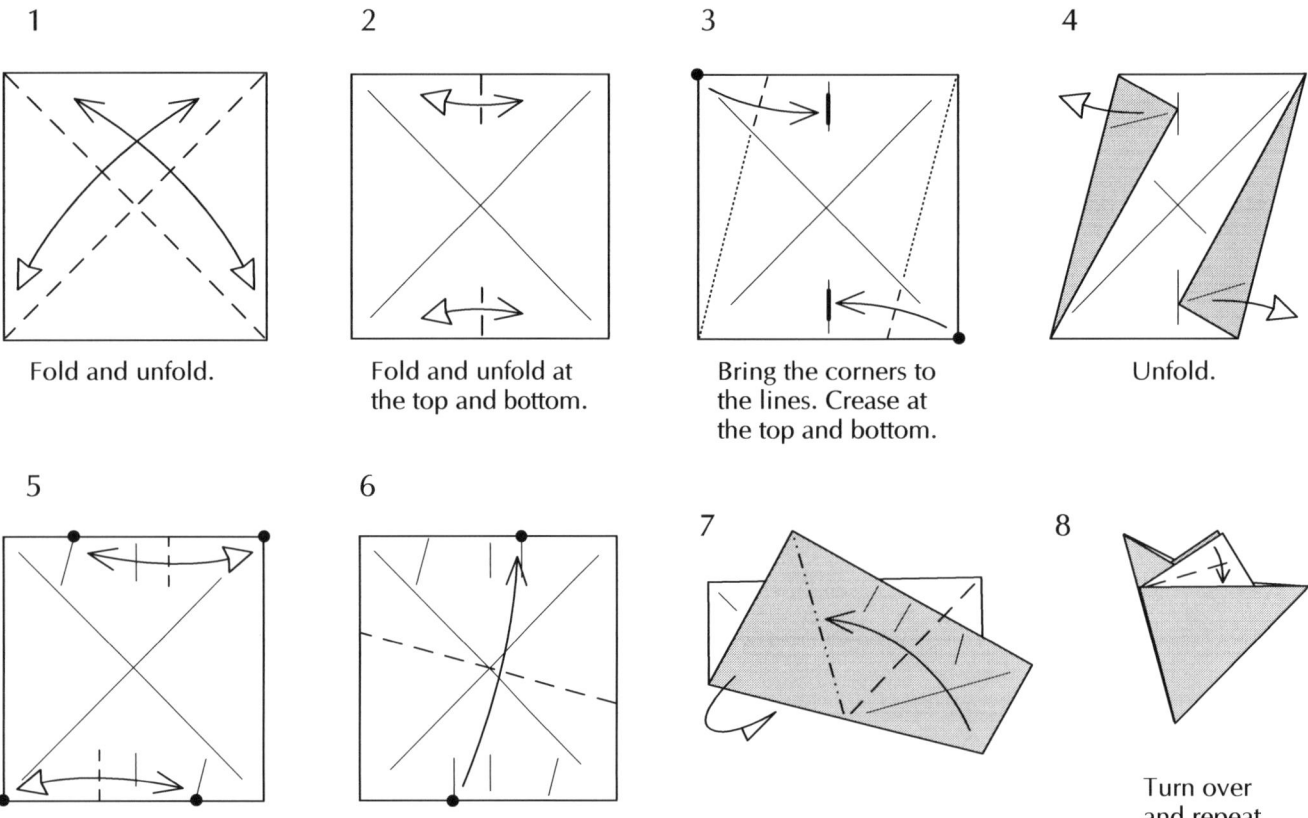

1. Fold and unfold.
2. Fold and unfold at the top and bottom.
3. Bring the corners to the lines. Crease at the top and bottom.
4. Unfold.
5. Fold and unfold at the top and bottom.
6. The dots will meet.
7.
8. Turn over and repeat.

18   *3D Origami Platonic Solids & More*

Octahedron (2)

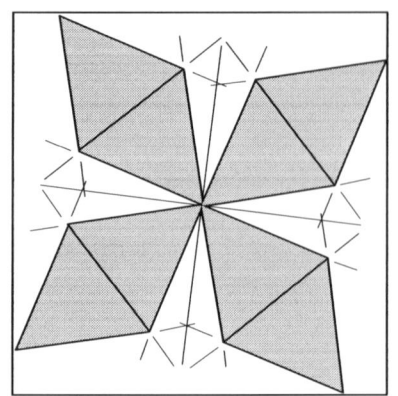

The design for this octahedron has square symmetry. The model closes with four thin tabs interlocking at the top, a concept called the twist lock. The thin tabs allow for efficient use of paper so this version is larger than the previous one.

1 Make small marks by folding and unfolding in half.

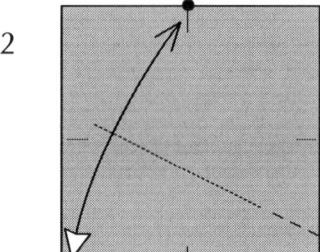

2 Fold and unfold on the right. Rotate 90°.

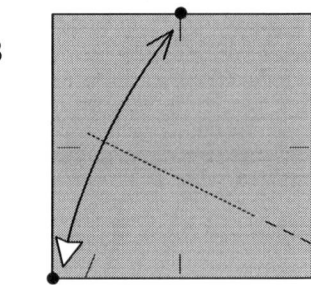

3 Repeat step 2 three more times.

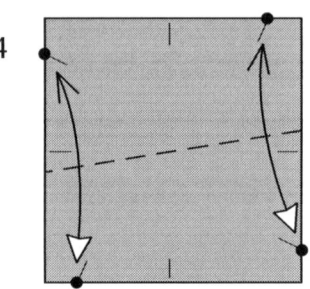

4 Bring the pair of dots together and unfold. Rotate 90°.

5 Fold and unfold.

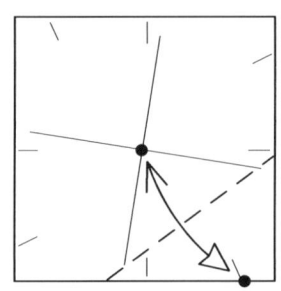

6 Fold and unfold. Rotate 90°.

20   *3D Origami Platonic Solids & More*

7

Repeat step 6 three more times.

8

Fold and unfold on the right. Rotate 90°.

9

Repeat step 8 three more times.

10

Fold and unfold on the left. Rotate 90°.

11

Repeat step 10 three more times.

12

Fold and unfold.

13

Fold and unfold.

14

15

Unfold.

16

Repeat steps 14–15 three more times.

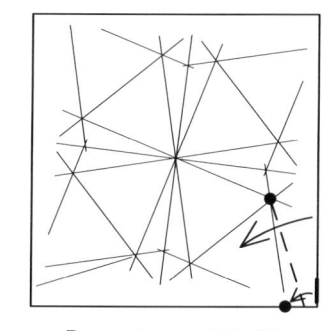

17

Push in at the dot.

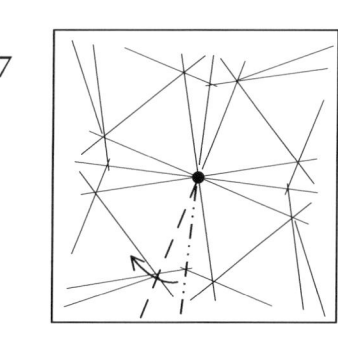

18

Squash-fold to form a triangle.

Octahedron 21

19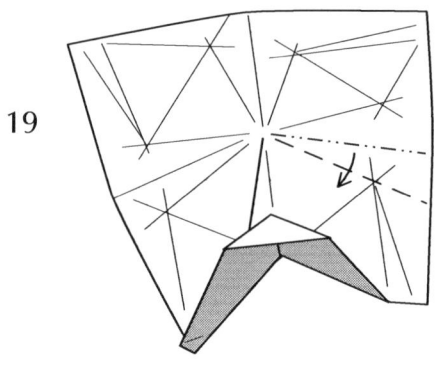

The orientation of the white triangle is not important. Repeat steps 17–18 three more times. Rotate to view the outside.

20

Flatten.

21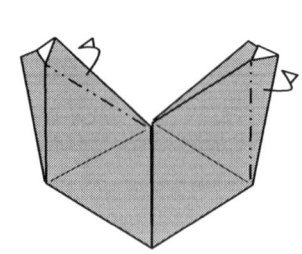

Turn over and repeat.

22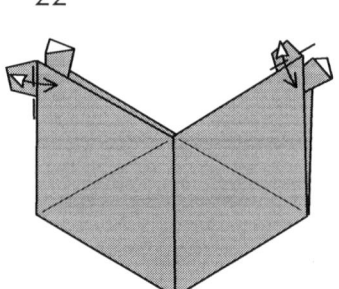

Fold and unfold. Repeat behind.

23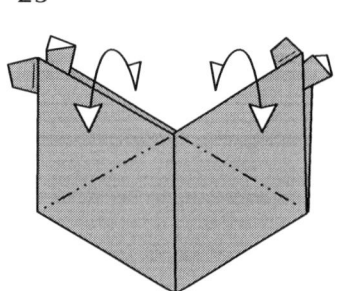

Open to fold inside and unfold. Do not flatten. Repeat behind.

24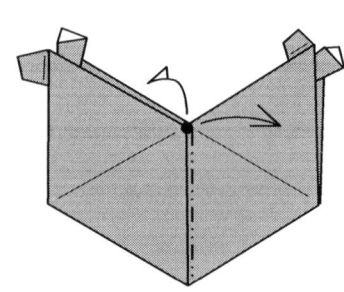

Open and flatten. Follow the dot in the next step.

25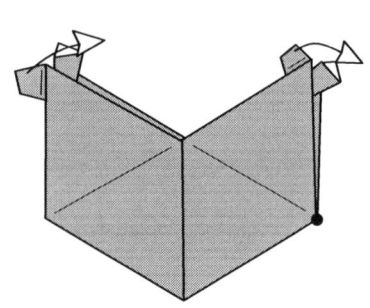

Unfold the thin flaps. Repeat behind.

26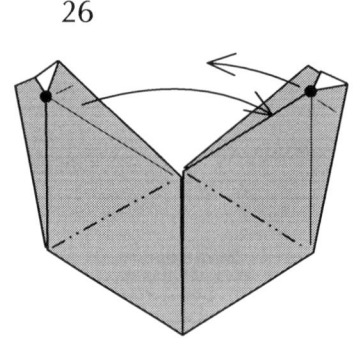

Close the model by interlocking the four tabs. The tabs spiral inward. This method is called a twist lock.

27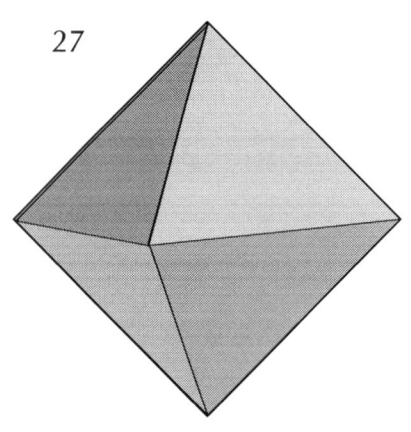

Octahedron

22   3D Origami Platonic Solids & More

Icosahedron

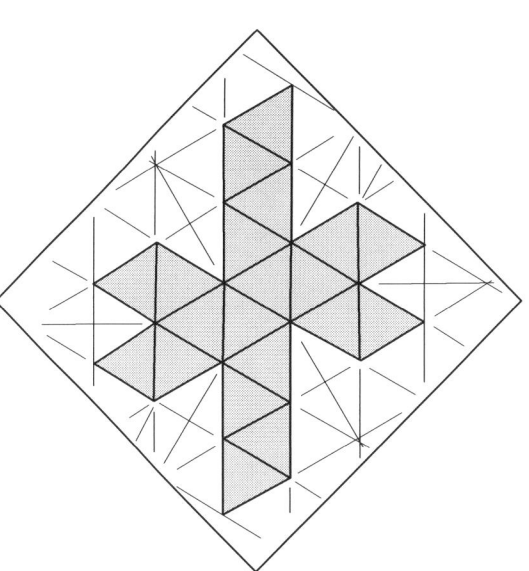

The icosahedron is composed of 20 equilateral triangles. Plato attributed this model to water because if its ability to roll.

The layout shows a band of ten triangles down the diagonal with five triangles on each side. Odd symmetry is used.

1

Fold and unfold on the left and right.

2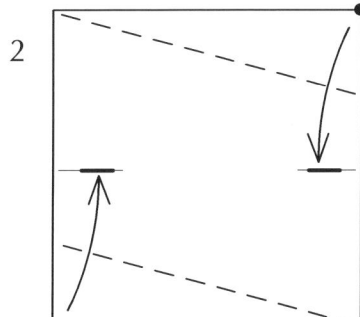

Bring the corners to the lines.

3

Fold in half.

4

Unfold.

5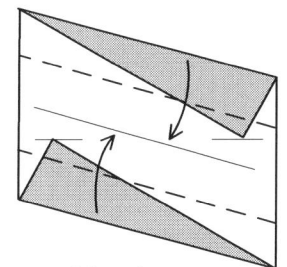

Fold to the center.

6

Unfold.

7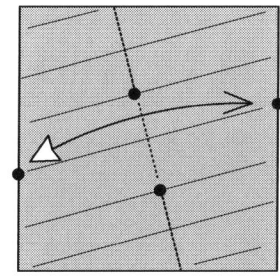

Fold and unfold at the top and bottom. Turn over and rotate.

8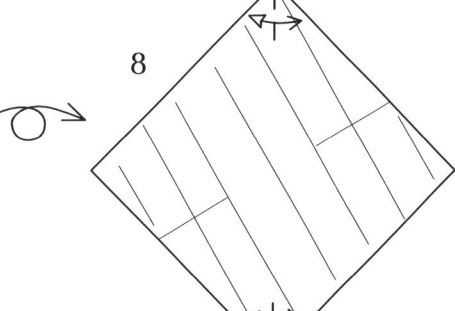

Fold and unfold at the ends.

9

Icosahedron 23

21

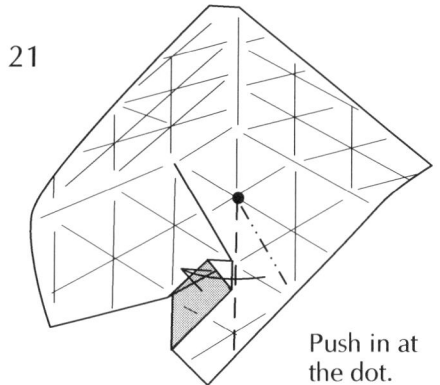

Push in at the dot.

22

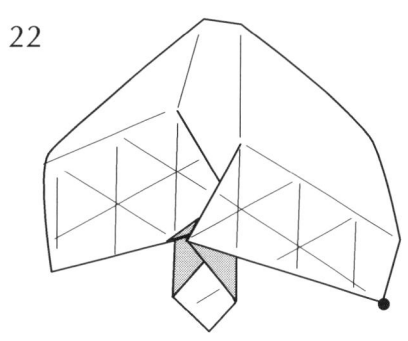

Repeat steps 19–21 on the other side. Rotate to view the outside so the dot is in front and at the top.

23

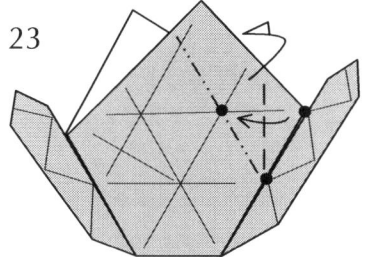

Puff out at the lower dot.

24

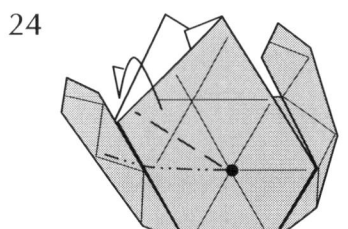

Puff out at the dot.

25

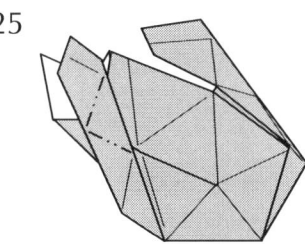

Mountain-fold along the band to reinforce the creases. Fold and unfold.

26

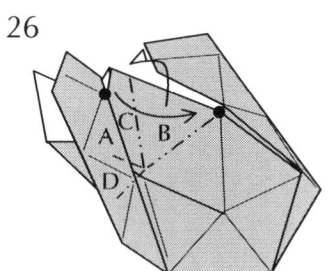

Triangle A will cover triangle B. Region C will go under D. The dots will meet.

27

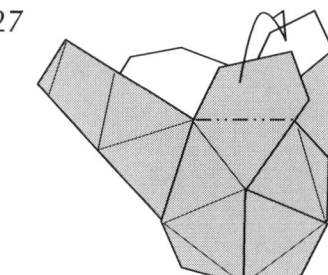

Tuck inside by wrapping around the layers.

28

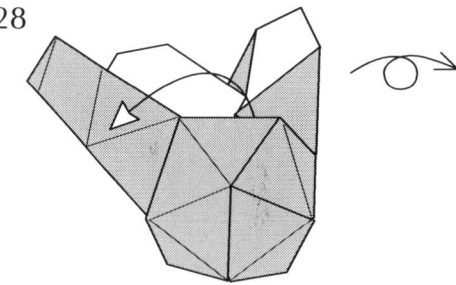

Unfold back to step 23.

29

Repeat steps 23–27.

30

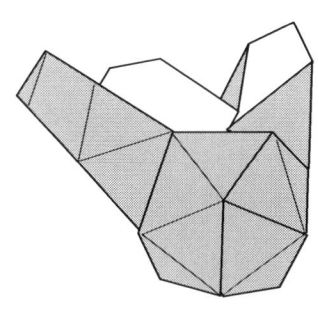

Refold steps 23–27 behind.

31

Icosahedron

Dodecahedron

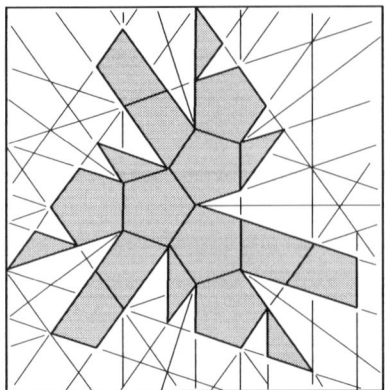

The dodecahedron has twelve pentagonal faces. To Plato, the dodecahedron, the quintessence (the "fifth being"), represented the whole universe.

This was a formidable model to design. I must have made a plethora of different versions before selecting this one to diagram. To simplify the folding, I allowed some faces to have lines through them. This method uses a minimal amount of folding (though plenty of precreasing). A version of the dodecahedron with clean faces can be found in *Classic Polyhedra Origami*.

1
Fold and unfold.

2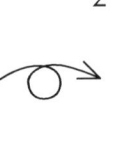
Fold and unfold on the left.

3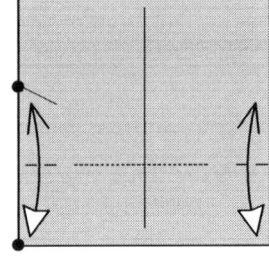
Fold and unfold on the edges.

4

5
Fold and unfold.

6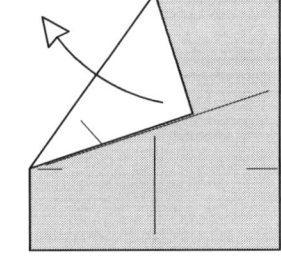
Unfold.

26   *3D Origami Platonic Solids & More*

Dodecahedron

26

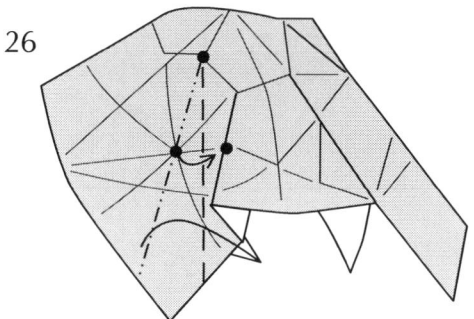

Puff out at the upper dot. Mountain-fold along the crease so the lower dots meet.

27

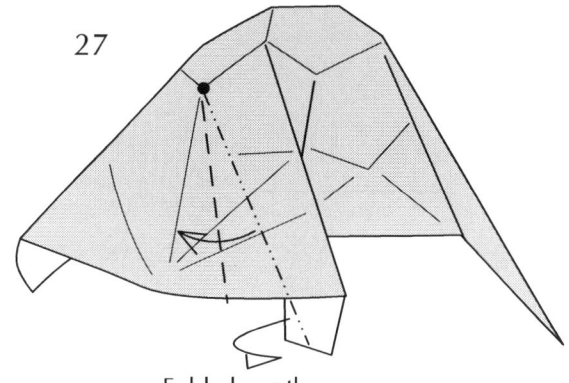

Fold along the creases and puff out at the dot.

28

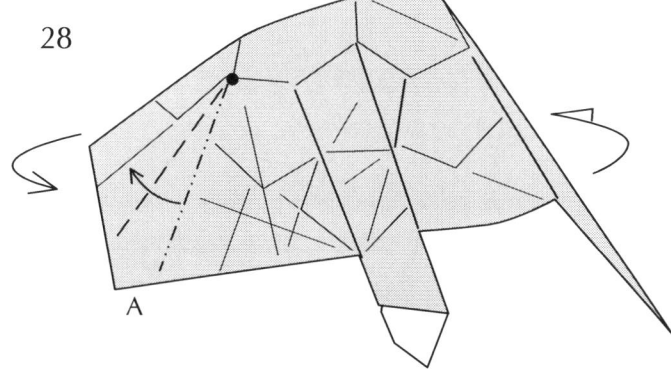

Note corner A. Fold along the creases and puff out at the dot. Rotate so the dot goes towards the center.

29

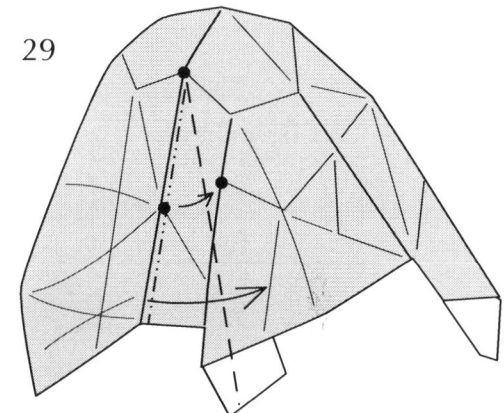

Puff out at the upper dot. Mountain-fold along the crease so the lower dots meet.

30

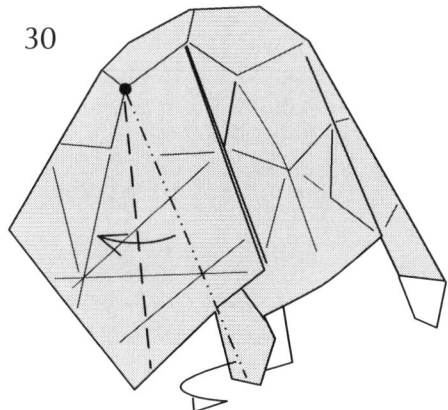

Fold along the creases and puff out at the dot.

31

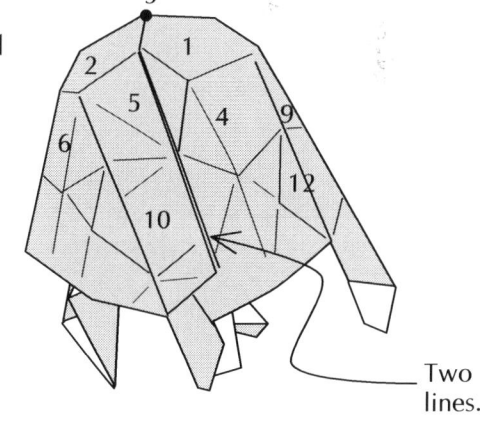

Two lines.

In this picture, the vertex at the dot is at the top. The vertex meets the top three pentagons, labeled 1, 2, and 3. Pentagon 3 is on the back. Below these three are six going around, labeled 4, 5, 6, ... , 9. Pentagons 7 and 8 are behind. (9 is just barely visible on the right.) By the bottom are the last three pentagons—10, 11, 12. 11 is behind. Also, there are two lines at the same location going down on pentagons 5 and 10, and this happens only once. Rotate so the vertex at the dot becomes the bottom, and the 2 lines are showing in front on the left.

Dodecahedron 29

32

Fold and unfold.

33

Fold and unfold.

34

Bring the dots together by folding tabs A and B toward each other. The three lower dots will meet and the two upper ones will meet. Tab A will tuck under B.

35

Unfold to step 32, then repeat steps 32–34, unfold back to step 32, and repeat steps 32–34 once again, each time on a different side. Tabs A, B, and C interlock as if they are three interwoven ribbons. As you go around to repeat these steps, the edges and tabs are all a bit different, but the same folding process is used. Since tab A is the shortest one, it is easiest to tuck that one in last.

There are three sides where the last tabs were tucked inside, it is possible to inflate into one of these sides to round out the dodecahedron.

36

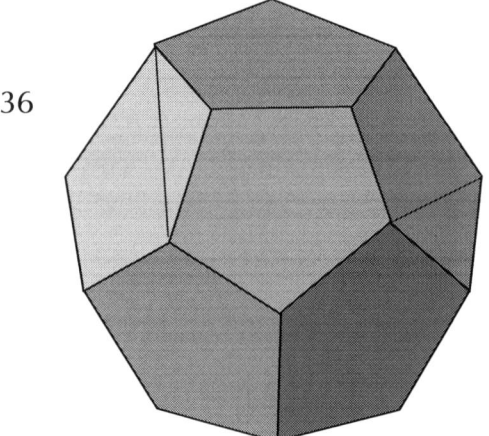

Dodecahedron

Sunken Platonic Solids

The shapes of the five sunken Platonic solids are variations of the regular solids. Each face of the regular solid is divided into several isosceles triangles which indent towards the center of the model.

The sunken Platonic solids are nonconvex polyhedra. For each model, the faces are identical isosceles triangles.

This imaginative set makes for a beautiful and powerful display. The folding methods for each of these challenging models are amazingly different.

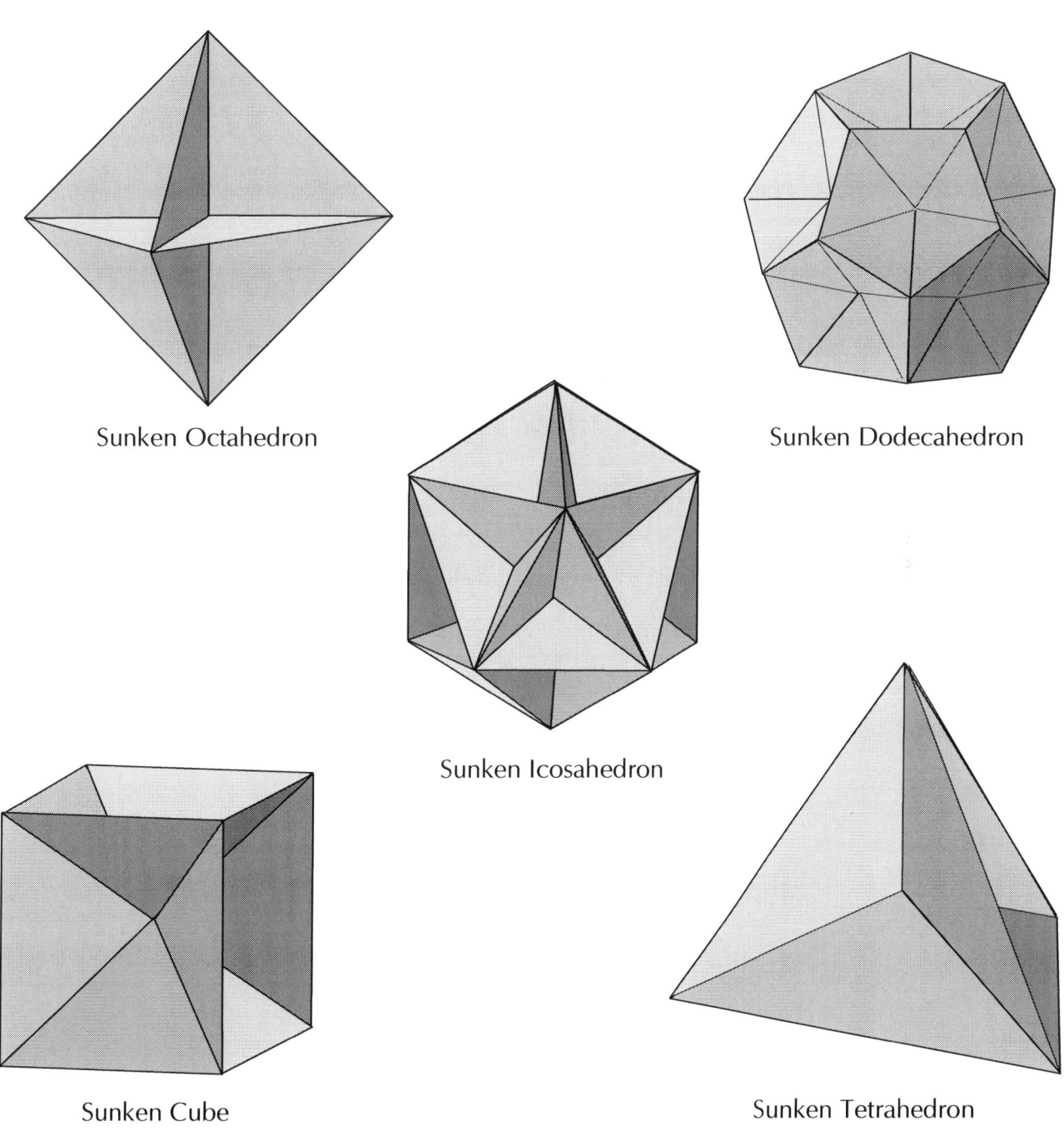

Sunken Octahedron

Sunken Dodecahedron

Sunken Icosahedron

Sunken Cube

Sunken Tetrahedron

Sunken Octahedron

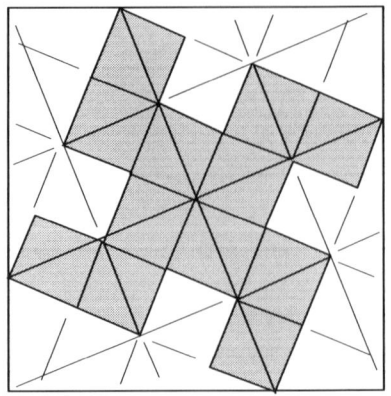

All the faces meet at the center, and this model can be viewed as three intersecting squares in three dimensions. Square symmetry is used.

1

Fold and unfold.

2

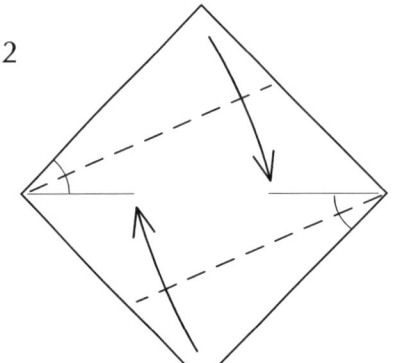

Fold to the center.

3

Fold in half.

4

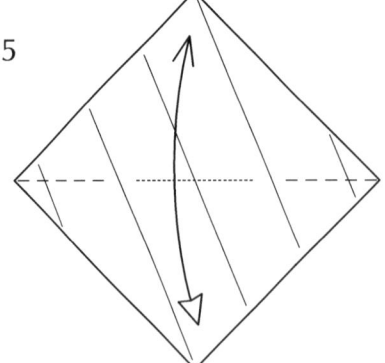

Unfold and rotate 90°.

5

Repeat steps 1–4.

6

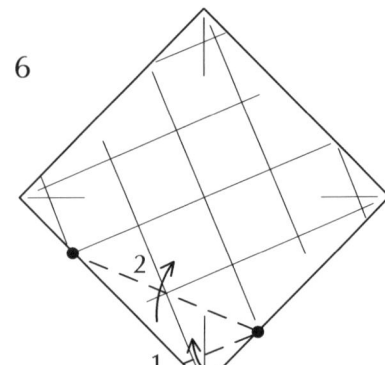

1. Fold along the crease.
2. Fold by the dots.
Rotate 90°.

32   *3D Origami Platonic Solids & More*

7

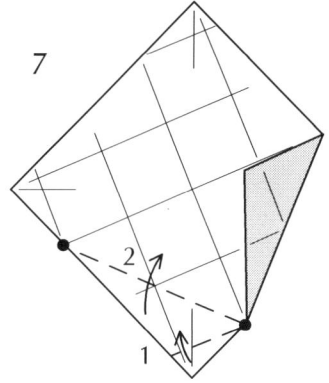

Repeat step 6 three times. Rotate.

8

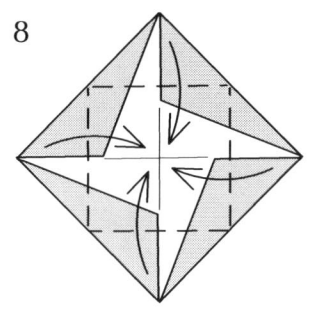

Fold along the creases.

9

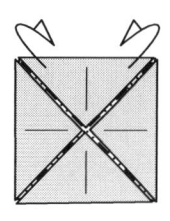

Fold and unfold. Rotate.

10

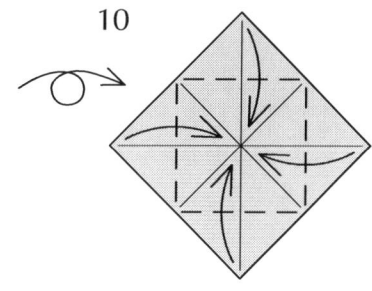

Fold to the center.

11

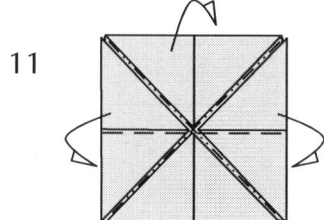

Fold along the creases. It is easier to do steps 11 and 12 as one step.

12

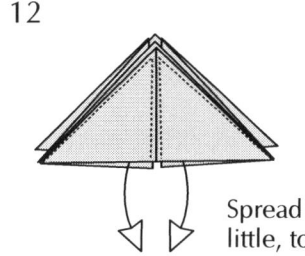

Spread the paper a little, to pull out the flaps. Repeat behind.

13

Pull out.

14

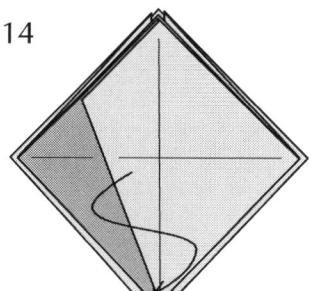

Tuck under the dark layer.

15

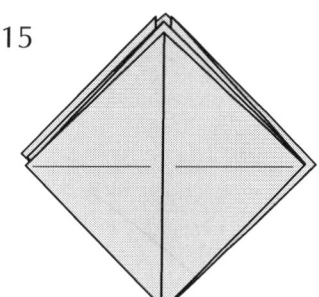

Repeat steps 13–14 three times, on the back and sides.

16

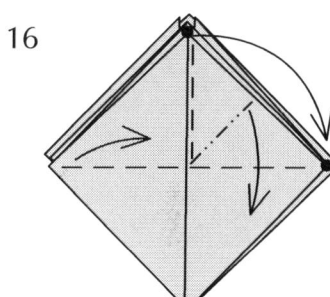

Bring the dots together and lift up on the left. The model will become 3D.

17

Tuck inside.

18

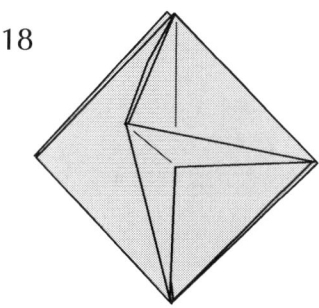

Repeat steps 16–17 on the three remaining sides.

19

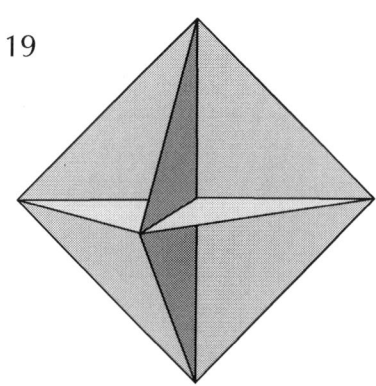

Sunken Octahedron

Sunken Tetrahedron

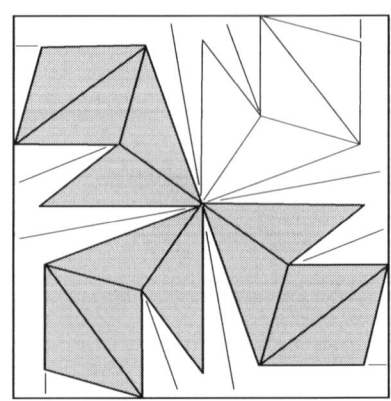

The twelve faces of the sunken tetrahedron are isosceles triangles. The sides of each triangular face are proportional to $2\sqrt{2}$, $\sqrt{3}$, and $\sqrt{3}$. The crease pattern shows 3/4 square symmetry.

1. Fold and unfold.

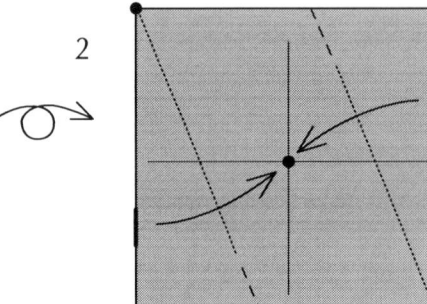

2. Bring the edges to the center creasing on the edges.

3. Unfold.

4. Fold and unfold.

5.

6.
1. Fold along the crease.
2. Fold along a hidden crease.

34   *3D Origami Platonic Solids & More*

Suken Tetrahedron 35

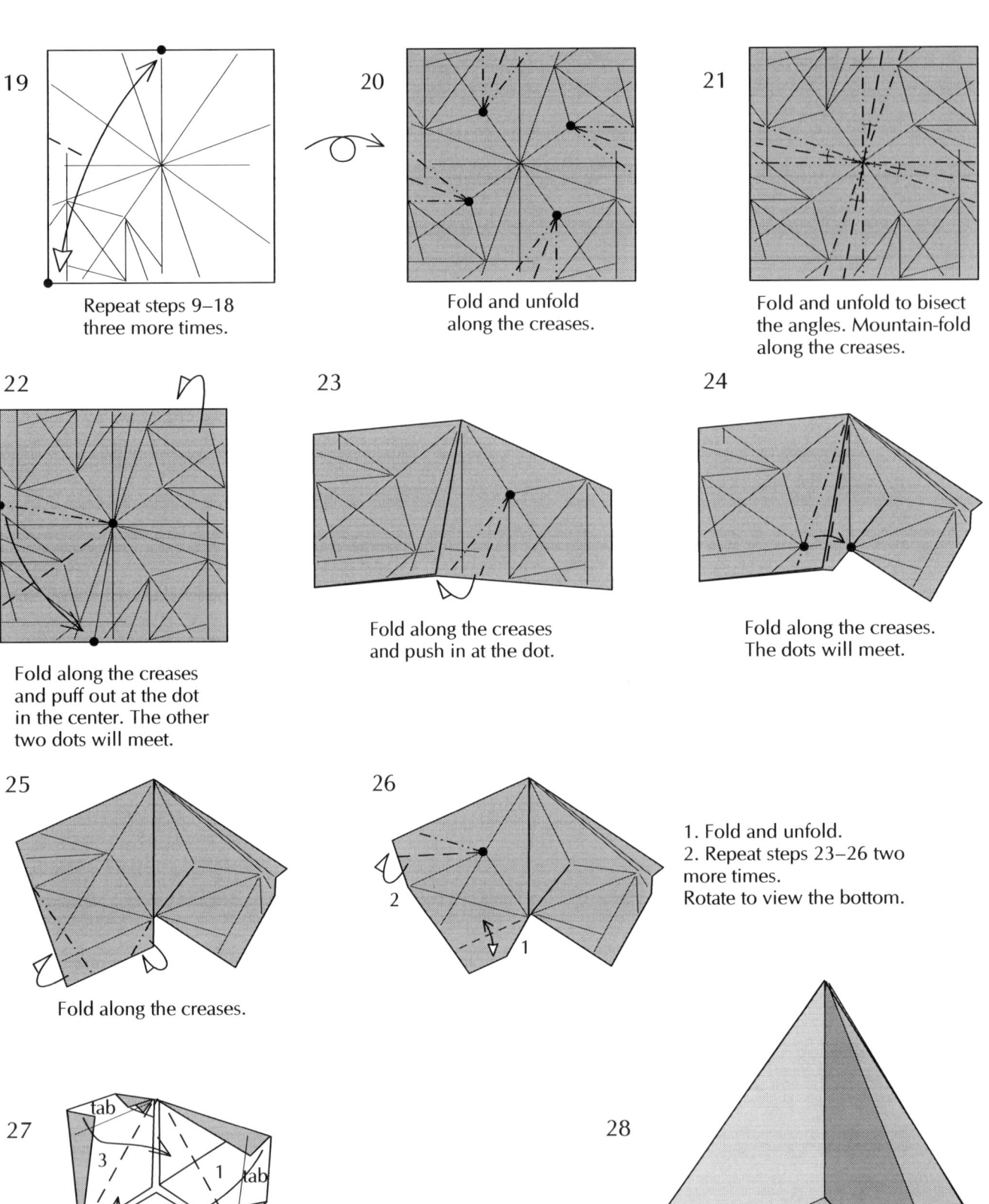

Sunken Tetrahedron

Sunken Cube

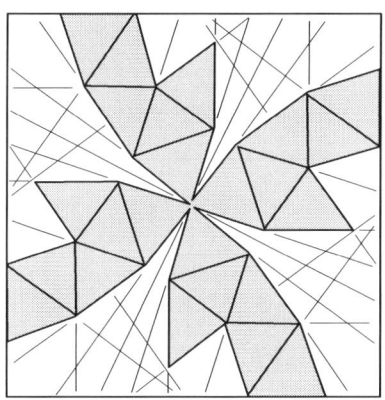

The sunken cube is composed of 24 isosceles triangles all meeting at the center. Each face has sides proportional to 1, $\sqrt{3}$, and $\sqrt{3}$. The crease pattern shows square symmetry.

1

Make small marks by folding and unfolding in half.

2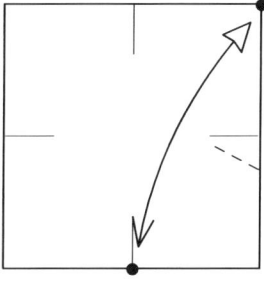

Fold and unfold on the right.

3

Fold and unfold. Rotate 90°.

4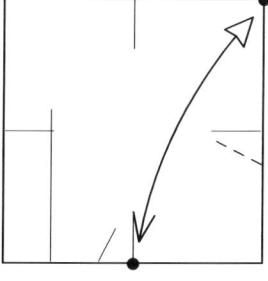

Repeat steps 2–3 three times.

5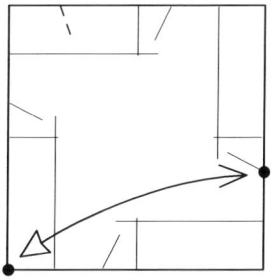

Fold and unfold at the top.

6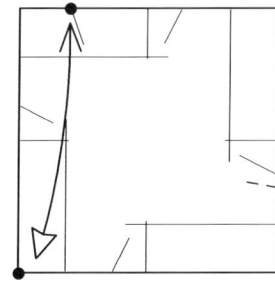

Fold and unfold on the right. Rotate 180°.

Sunken Cube 37

19

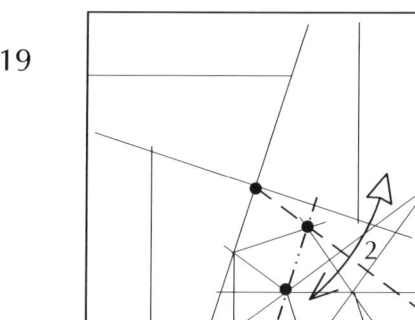

1. Fold behind and unfold along the crease by two dots.
2. Fold and unfold by the dot in the center of the square. Rotate 90°.

20

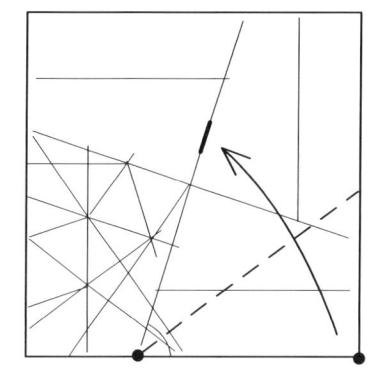

Repeat steps 10–19 three times.

21

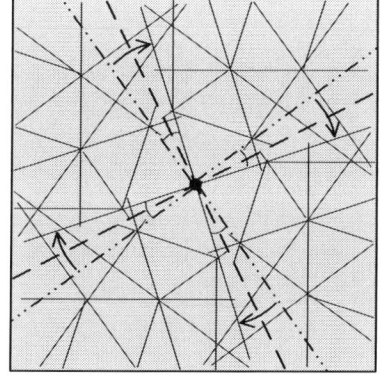

Bisect the angles. Mountain-fold along the creases. Puff out at the dot.

22

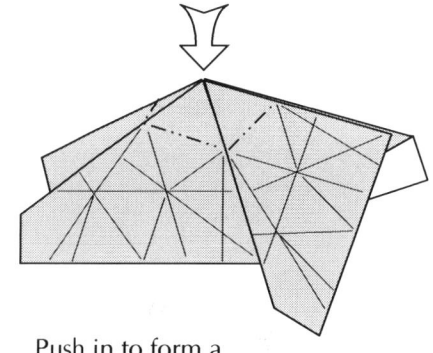

Push in to form a sunken square. Rotate the top to the bottom.

23

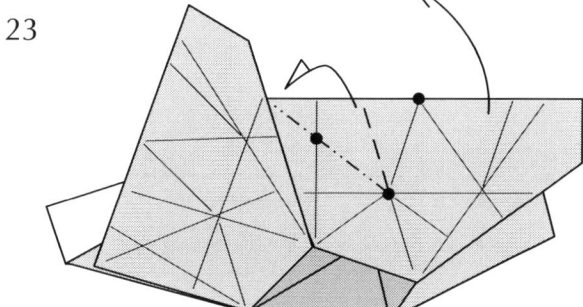

Push in at the lower dot. The other two dots will meet.

24

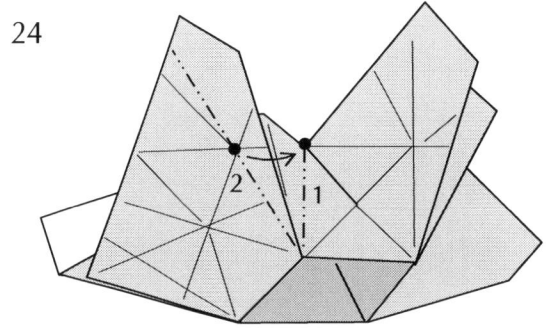

1. Fold and unfold along the crease.
2. Slide the paper so the dots meet.

Sunken Cube 39

25

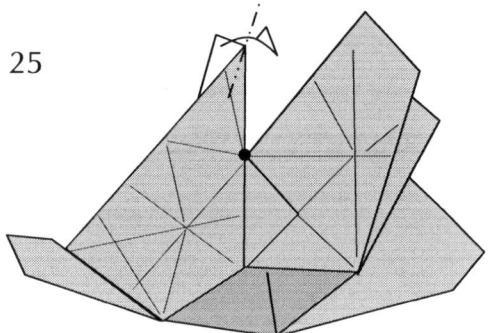

Fold the tab behind so the edge meets the dot.

26

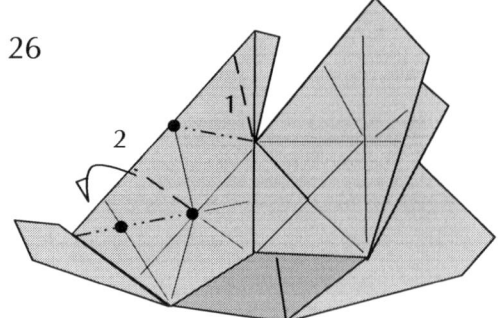

1. Fold and unfold along the creases.
2. Repeat steps 23–26 three times.

27

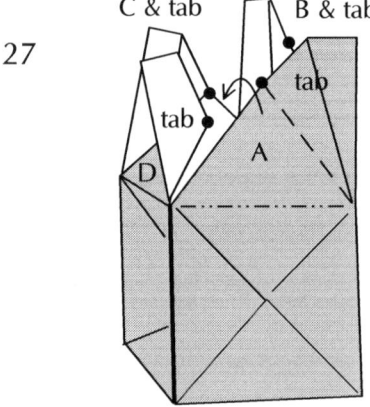

Fold region A down towards the center. Fold B down to cover A's tab. Fold C down to cover B's tab. Fold D down and tuck its tab under A to form a sunken square on top and close the model.

28

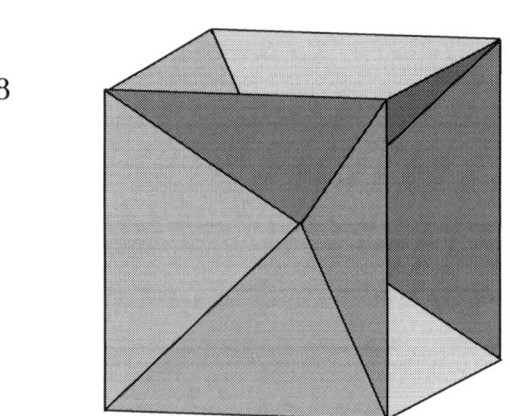

Sunken Cube

Sunken Dodecahedron

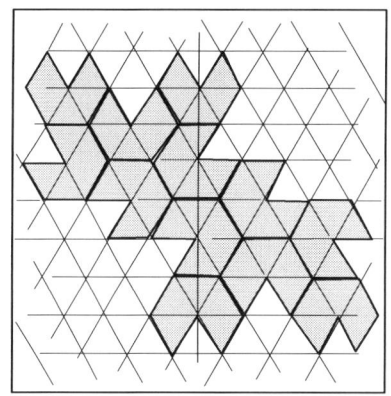

This sunken dodecahedron is one of several stellated icosahedra. It is composed of 60 equilateral triangular faces. After the 1/5 mark is found in step 3, much precreasing is used to make many triangles. This sunken polyhedron was actually much easier to design than the dodecahedron itself.

1

Fold and unfold.

2

Crease on the ends.

3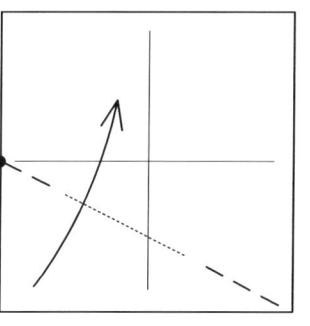

The paper is divided into fifths.

4

Unfold.

5

Fold and unfold.

6

Sunken Dodecahedron 41

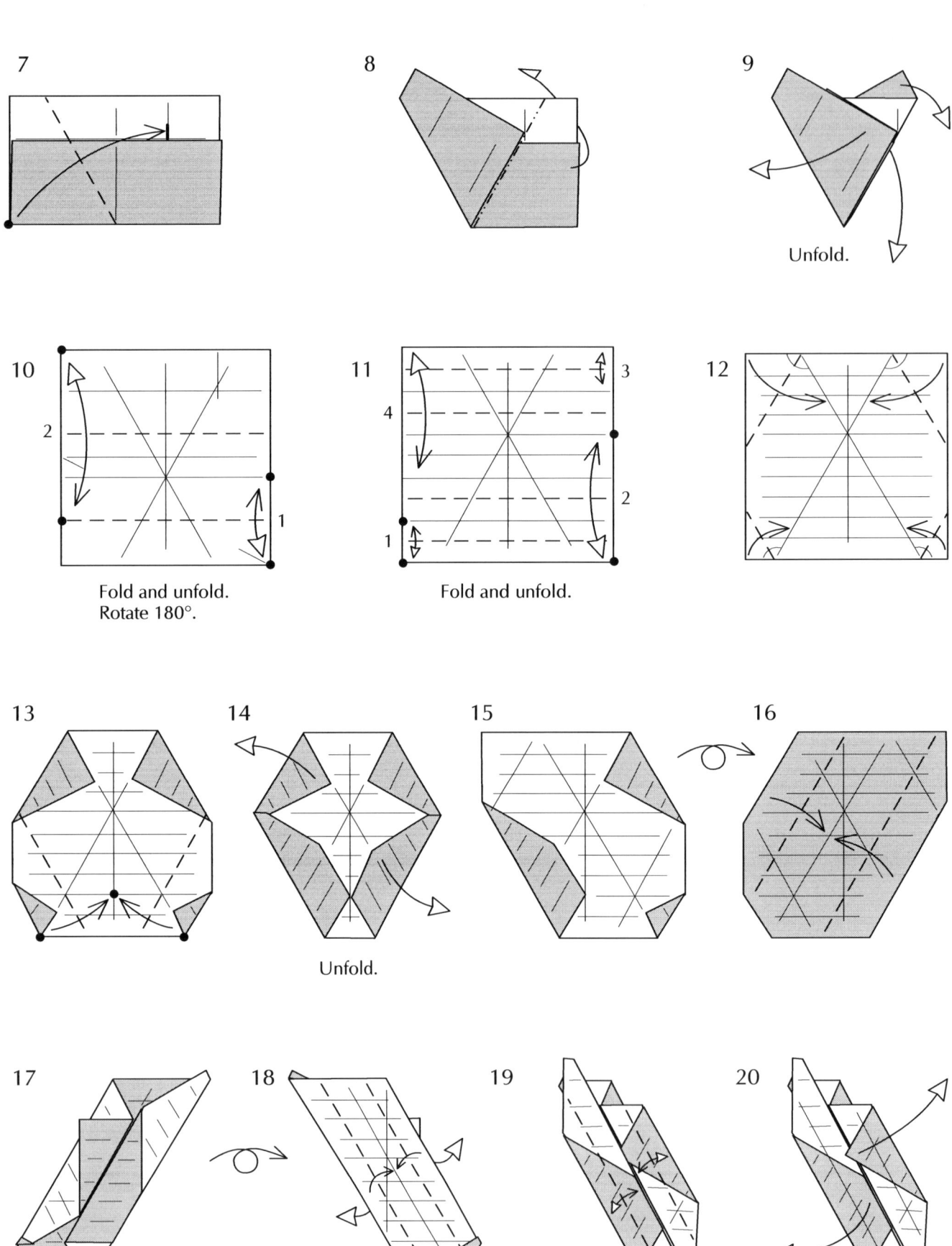

42 3D Origami Platonic Solids & More

Sunken Dodecahedron 43

Sunken Icosahedron

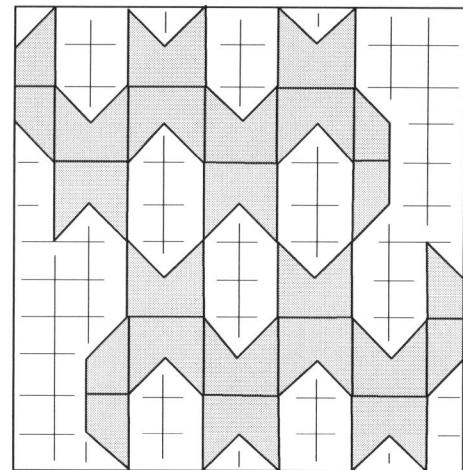

This complex shape is composed of 60 isosceles right triangular faces. It is formed by first making a fan. It has a four-star (very complex) rating because of the sequence from steps 20–33 as the fan is turned into a tower. But the folds before and after are not so difficult. The paper is divided into twelfths. This shape is complex and does not hold together as well as the other models in this collection, you can choose nonstandard methods (such as tape) to keep it together.

1

Fold and unfold.

2

Fold and unfold.

3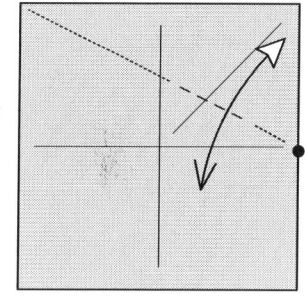

Fold and unfold along the diagonal.

4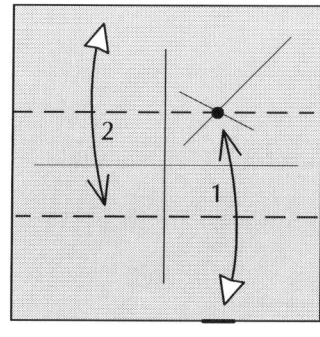

Fold and unfold. This divides the paper in thirds.

5

Fold and unfold.

6

Sunken Icosahedron 45

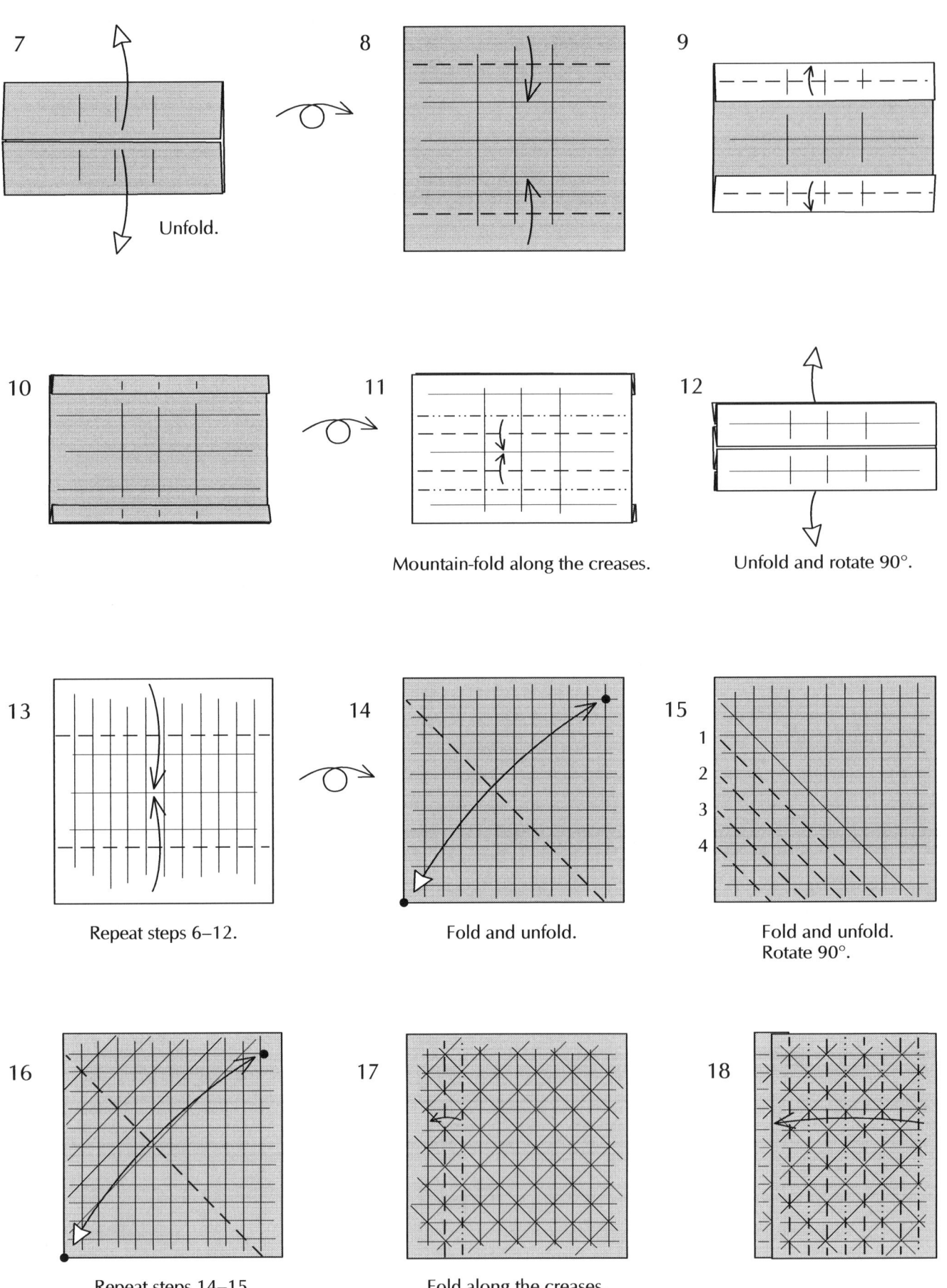

46 *3D Origami Platonic Solids & More*

19

20

Tuck into the lowest layer.

This is the most difficult part as the fan becomes a tower in step 34. Until then, the model will not hold together.

21

Rotate to view the left side.

22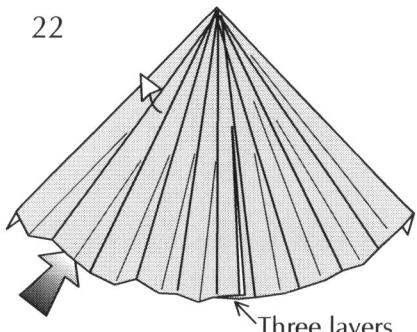

Pop out between the second and third bands.

Three layers

23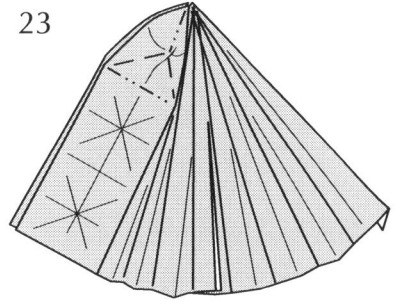

Make a sunken triangle along the creases.

24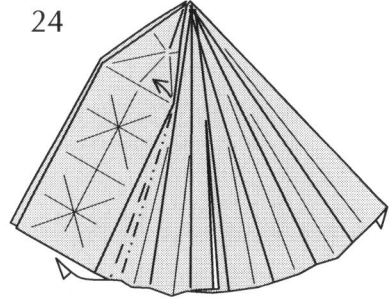

Wrap a layer underneath.

25

Repeat steps 22–24.

26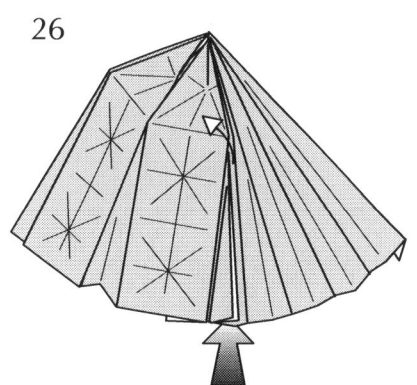

Repeat steps 22–24. This is where the edges meet.

27

Repeat steps 22–24.

28

29

Sunken Icosahedron 47

41

Fold all the loose edges going all around.

42

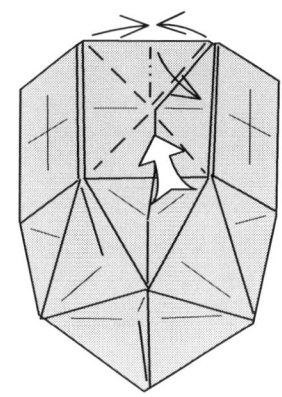

Form a sunken triangle bringing the extra paper to the front.

43

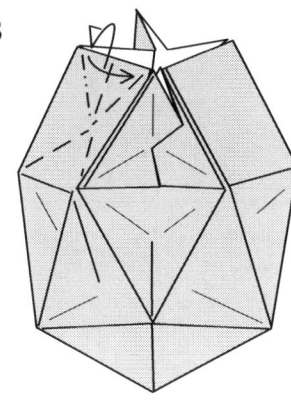

Form a sunken triangle while folding the extra paper inside.

44

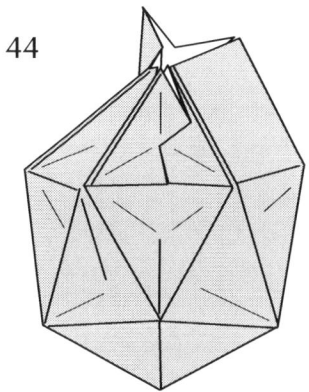

Repeat steps 43 on the right.

45

Form the last two triangles on the back while bringing the extra paper to the front inside the front triangle.

46

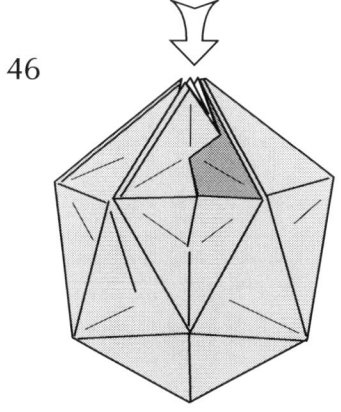

Bring the dark paper to the front to lock the folds. Also push down to keep the folds in place.

47

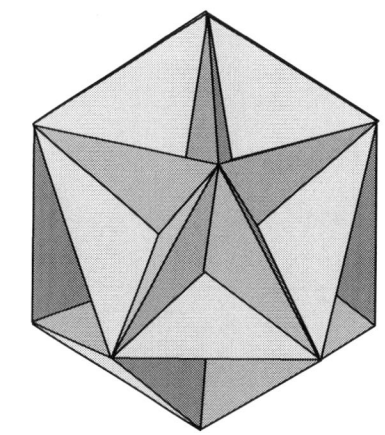

Sunken Icosahedron

Inside-Out Platonic Solids

Inside-out origami refers to models which show both sides of the paper for effect. To fold polyhedra with color patterns, the paper is first folded so both colors show on one side. Then a layout in 2D is placed. When folded, both sides are shown.

Consider the Three-Layered Cube. In figure 1, opposite edges are folded towards the center to show the colored side of the paper on the left and right, with a vertical white strip down the middle. The six squares are highlighted, showing each square with its color pattern. When folded into a cube, figure 2, the color pattern is realized.

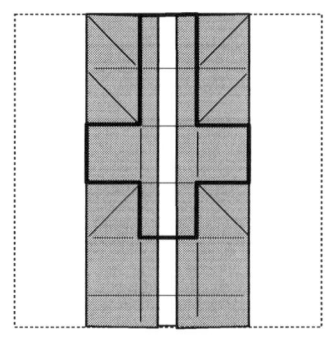

Figure 1: Layout of cube in 2D showing the set-up for the color pattern.

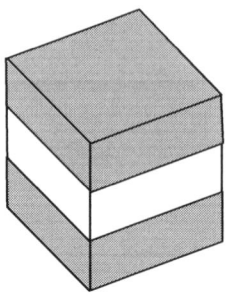

Figure 2: Cube with color pattern.

Duo-Striped Tetrahedron

Layered Tetrahedron

Three-Layered Cube

Fancy Cube

Banded Cube

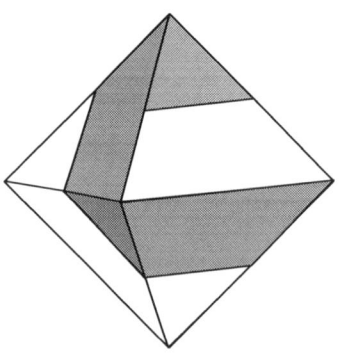

Banded Octahedron

Duo-Striped Tetrahedron

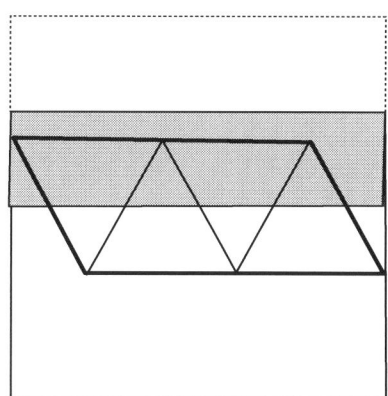

To fold this model, a striped cylinder is formed. With a few folds, the cylinder turns into the striped tetrahedron. The paper is divided into fifths.

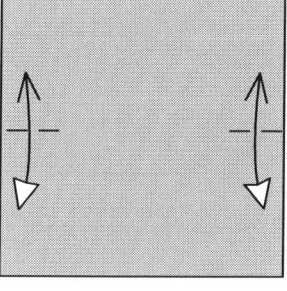

1. Fold and unfold on the left and right.

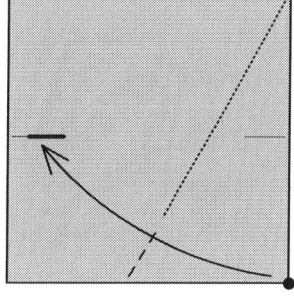

2. Crease at the bottom.

3. Unfold.

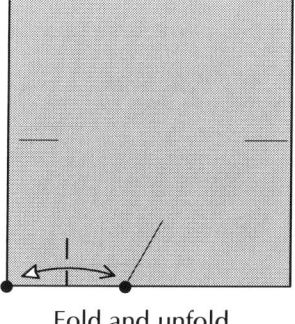

4. Fold and unfold. Rotate 180°.

5. Repeat steps 2–4.

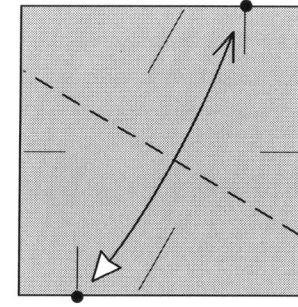

6. Fold and unfold.

Duo-Striped Tetrahedron 51

7

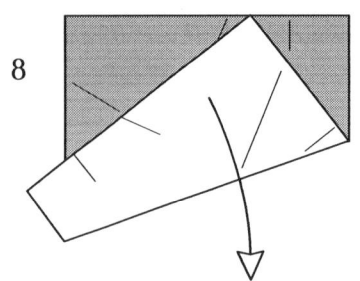

Bring the lower right corner to the top edge and the bottom edge to the left center. Crease on the right.

8

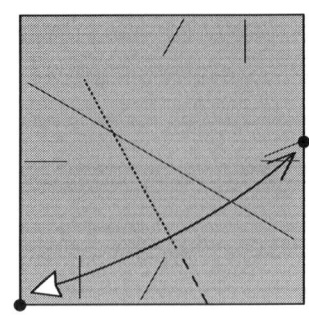

Unfold.

9

Fold and unfold at the bottom.

10

11

Fold and unfold along the crease.

12

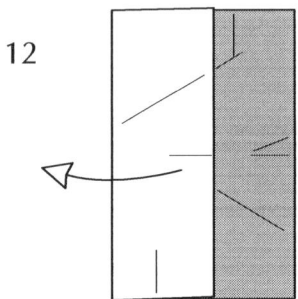

Unfold and rotate 180°.

13

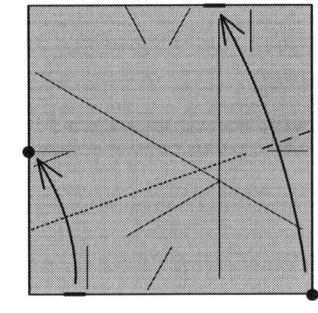

Repeat steps 7–12. Turn over and rotate 90°.

14

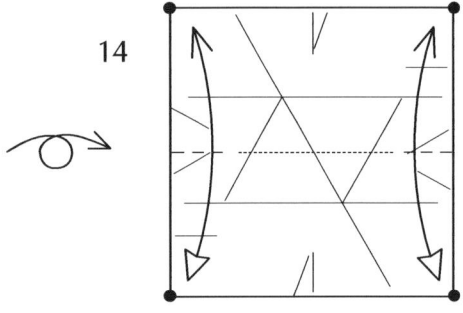

Fold and unfold at the edges.

15

16

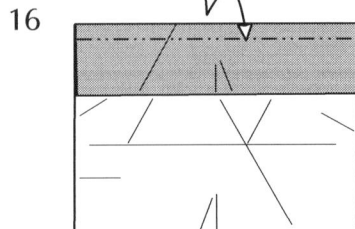

Fold and unfold along a hidden crease.

17

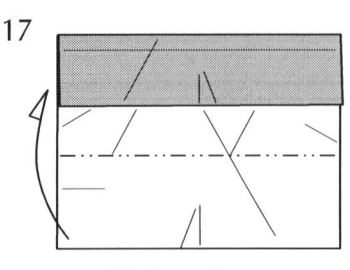

Fold along the crease.

18

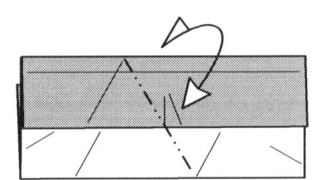

Fold and unfold all the layers along a partially hidden crease.

52   *3D Origami Platonic Solids & More*

19

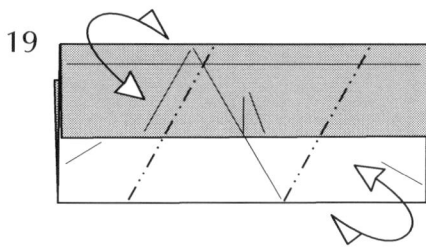

Fold and unfold all the layers along partially hidden creases.

20

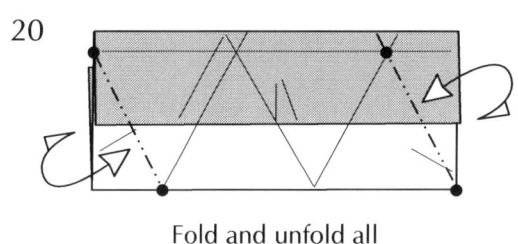

Fold and unfold all the layers together.

21

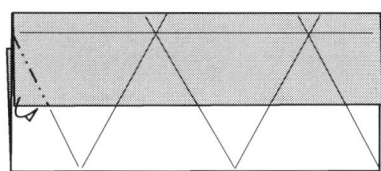

Fold along the crease.

22

Do not crease.

23

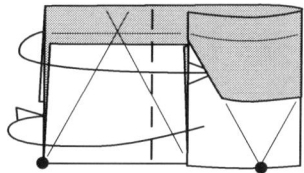

Tuck inside but do not crease. The dots will meet. Curl the model to make a cylinder.

24

25

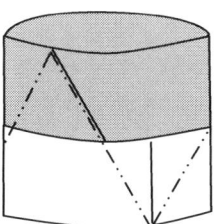

Turn the cylinder into a tetrahedron.

26

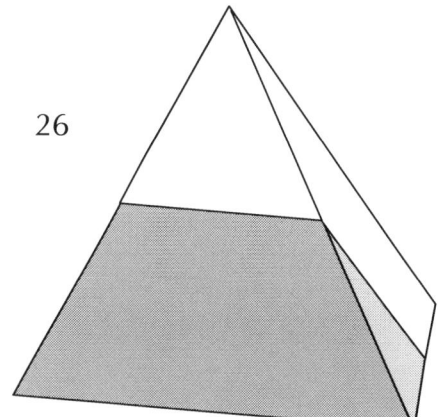

Duo-Striped Tetrahedron

Layered Tetrahedron

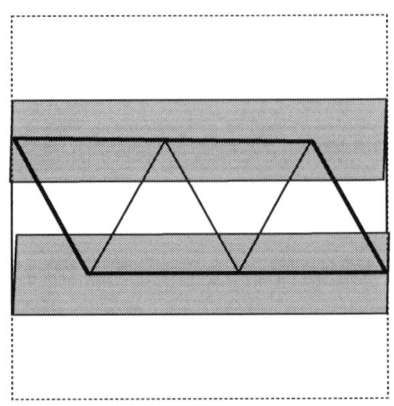

To fold this model, a striped cylinder is formed. With a few folds, the cylinder turns into the striped tetrahedron. The paper is divided into fifths.

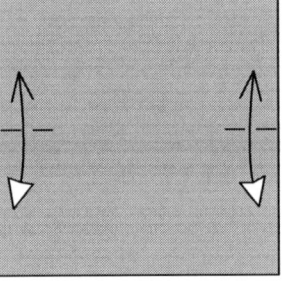

1. Fold and unfold on the left and right.

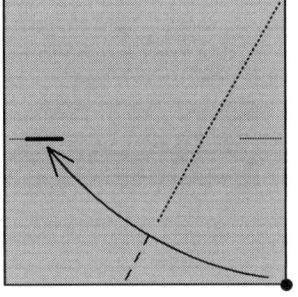

2. Crease at the bottom.

3. Unfold.

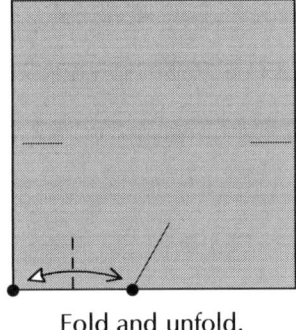

4. Fold and unfold. Rotate 180°.

5. Repeat steps 2–4.

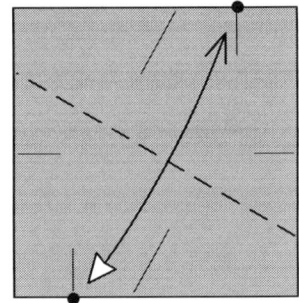

6. Fold and unfold.

54 *3D Origami Platonic Solids & More*

7

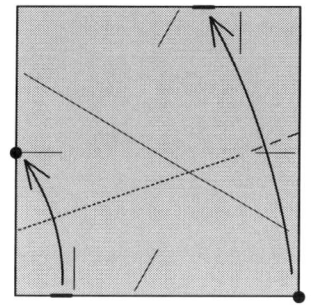

Bring the lower right corner to the top edge and the bottom edge to the left center. Crease on the right.

8

Unfold.

9

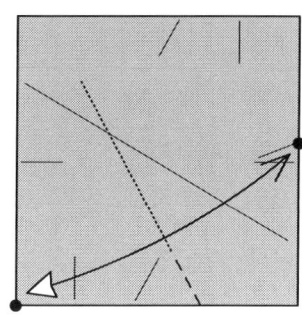

Fold and unfold at the bottom.

10

11

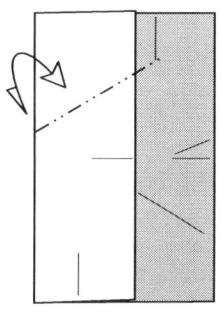

Fold and unfold along the crease.

12

Unfold and rotate 180°.

13

Repeat steps 7–12. Turn over and rotate 90°.

14

Fold and unfold at the edges.

15

16

17

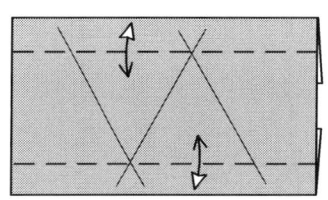

Fold and unfold all the layers together.

Layered Tetrahedron 55

18

Fold and unfold all the layers together.

19
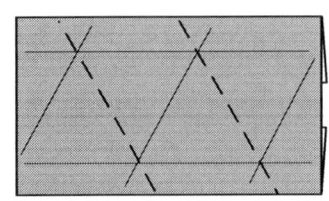
Fold and unfold all the layers together along the creases.

20

21

Do not crease.

22
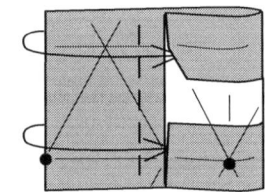
Tuck inside but do not crease. The dots will meet. Curl the model to make a cylinder.

23

24
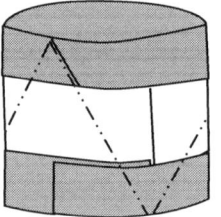
Turn the cylinder into a tetrahedron.

25
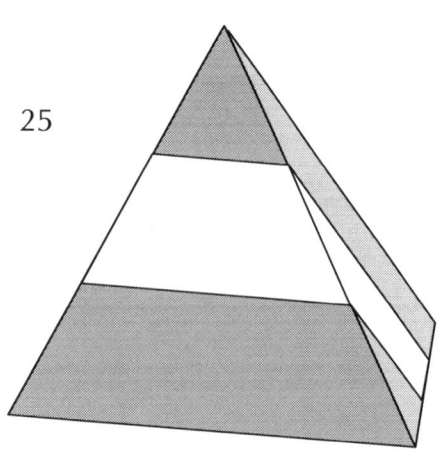

Layered Tetrahedron

56   *3D Origami Platonic Solids & More*

Three-Layered Cube

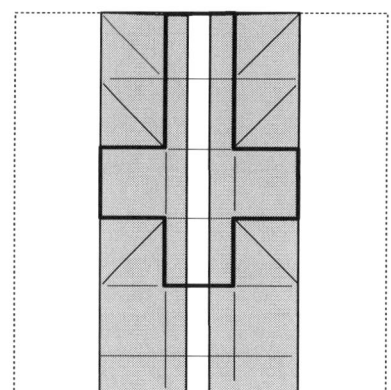

By folding opposite edges towards the center while leaving a white strip, a layout for the cube can be made that will result in this three-layered cube. The paper is divided into seventeenths. Even symmetry is used.

1

Fold and unfold on the left.

2

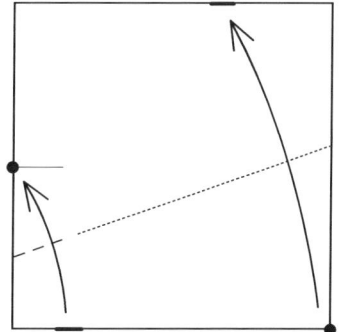

Bring the bottom right corner to the top and the bottom edge to the dot. Crease on the left.

3

Unfold.

4

The 2/9 mark is found. Fold and unfold so the dots meet. Rotate 180°.

5

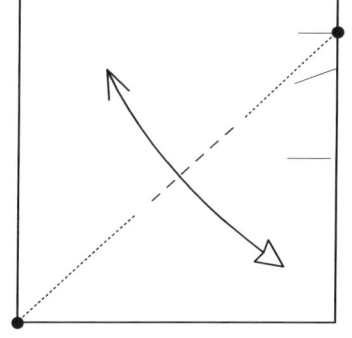

Fold and unfold in the center.

6

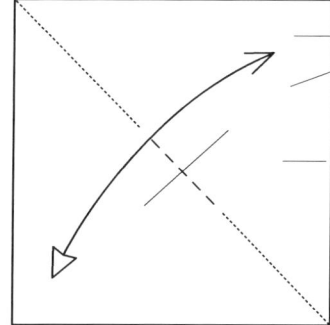

Fold and unfold in the center, along the diagonal.

Three-Layered Cube 57

7. Fold and unfold. 4/17

8. Fold and unfold in half, twice on the right.

9. Fold and unfold on the right.

10.
1. Fold to the dot.
2. Fold along the crease.

11. Fold and unfold along a crease that starts by the dot.

12. Fold and unfold.

13. Fold and unfold all the layers.

14. Fold and unfold all the layers.

15.

16. Fold along the hidden crease.

17. Unfold.

18. Fold and unfold.

58 *3D Origami Platonic Solids & More*

Three-Layered Cube 59

Fancy Cube

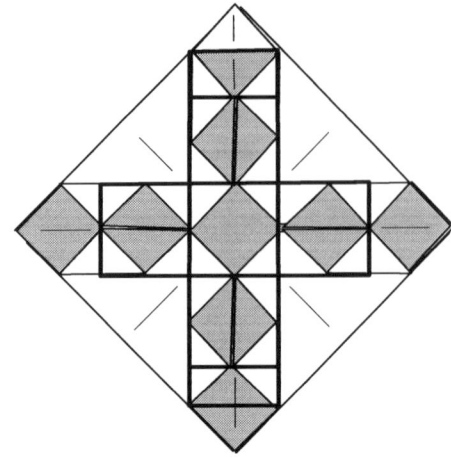

Each face of this cube has a diamond color pattern. The paper is divided into ninths. Square symmetry is used.

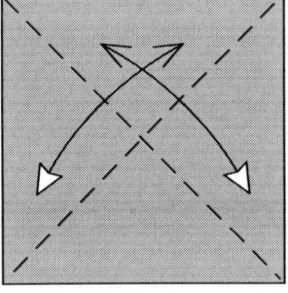

1. Fold and unfold along the diagonals.

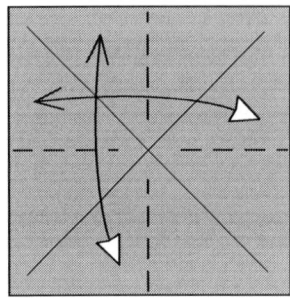

2. Fold and unfold but not in the center.

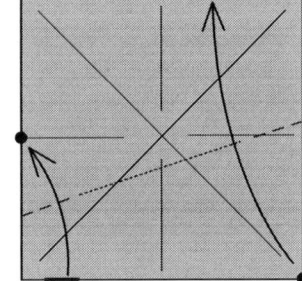

3. Bring the lower right corner to the top edge and the bottom edge to the left center. Crease on the left and right.

4. Unfold.

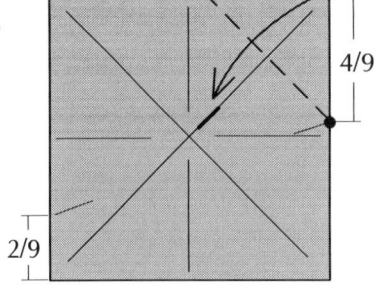

5. The 2/9 and 4/9 marks are found.

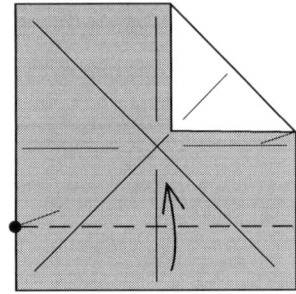

6.

60   *3D Origami Platonic Solids & More*

7

Squash-fold.

8

Squash-fold.

9

Squash-fold.

10

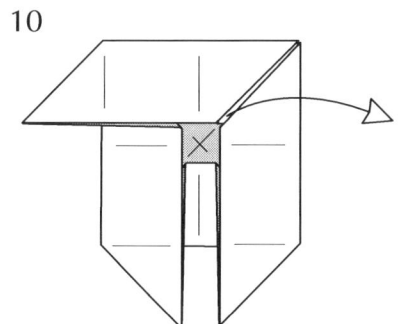

Pull out the hidden corner.

11

Squash-fold.

12

13

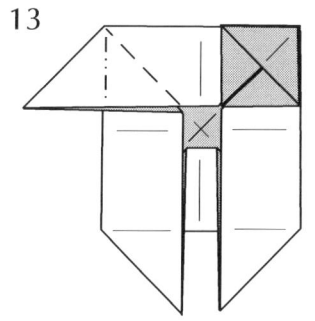

Repeat steps 11–12 on the three other corners.

14

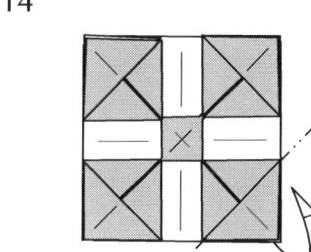

Turn over and rotate.

15

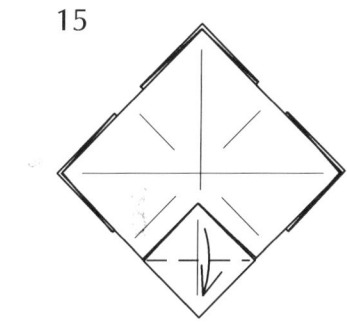

16

Repeat steps 14–15 three more times.

17

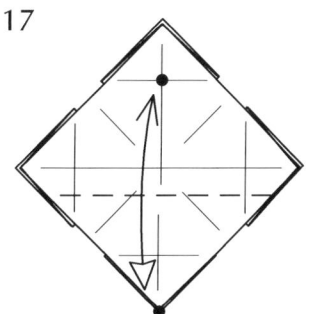

Fold and unfold. Rotate 90°.

18

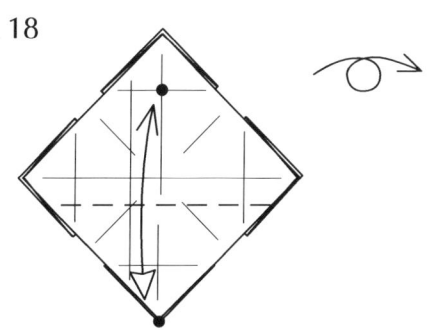

Repeat step 17 three more times.

Fancy Cube 61

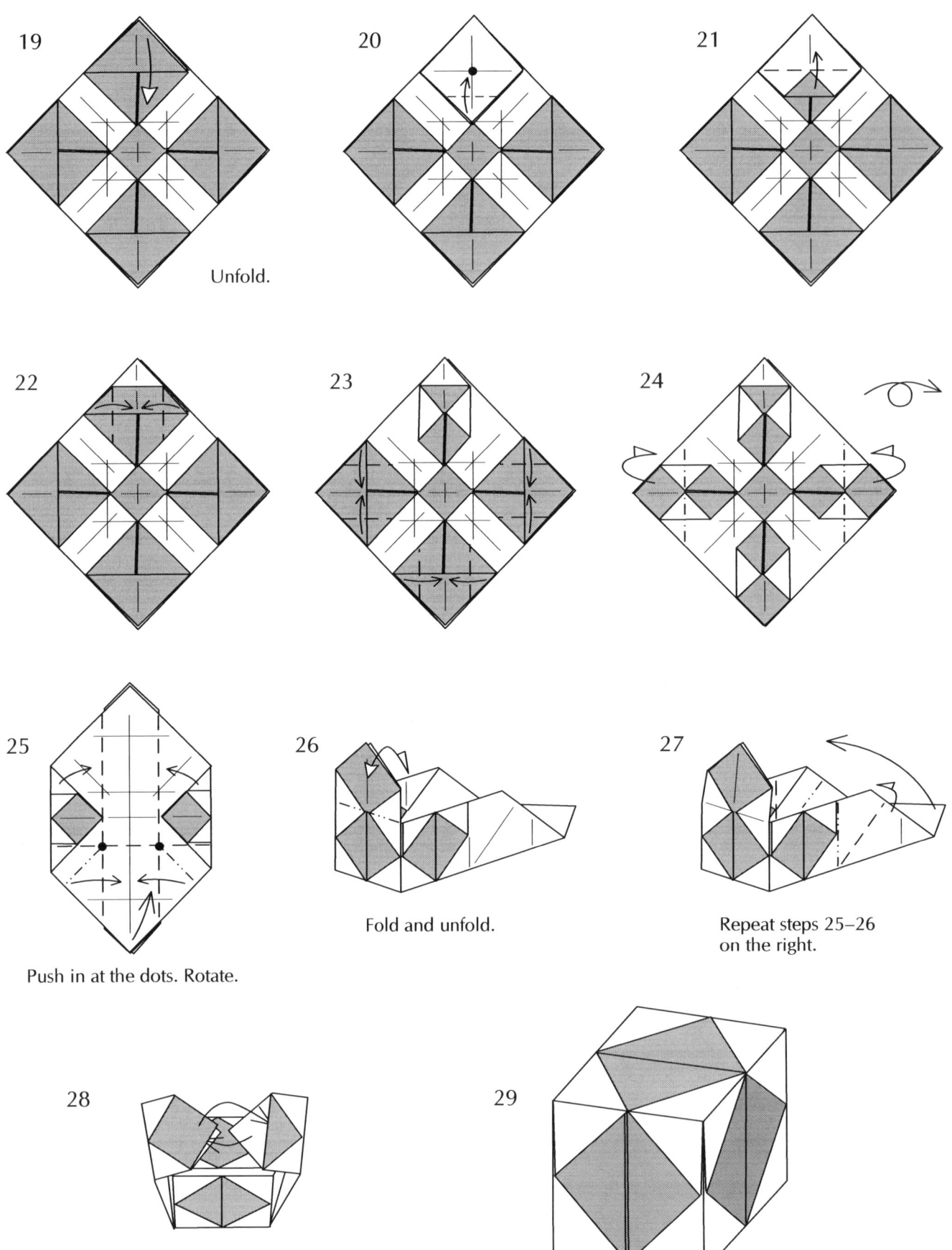

Fancy Cube

62 *3D Origami Platonic Solids & More*

Banded Cube

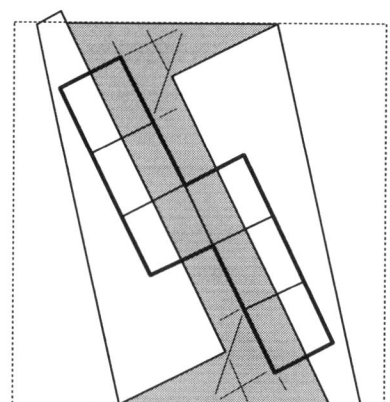

By folding two edges towards the center, a layout with stripes is formed. Placing the six square faces in two rows with three per row is an unusual way to contruct a cube. Odd symmetry is used.

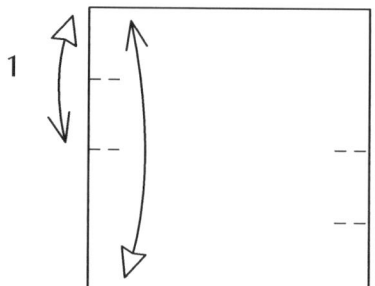

1. Make small marks by folding and unfolding in quarters.

2. Fold and unfold.

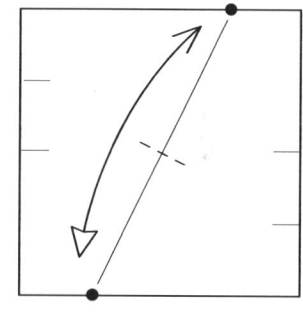

3. Fold and unfold in the center.

4.

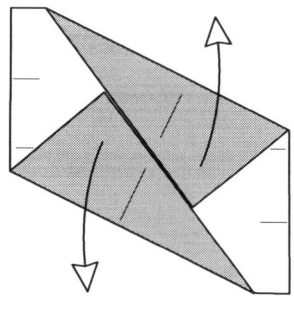

5. Unfold.

6. Fold and unfold.

Banded Cube   63

19. Fold and unfold.

20. Puff out at the dot.

21. Fold and unfold along the creases. Rotate.

22. Repeat steps 20–21.

23. Tuck inside.

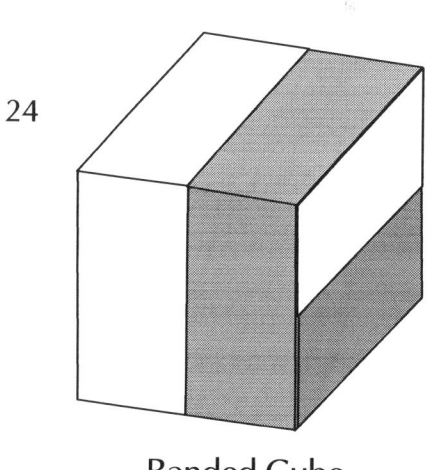

24.

Banded Cube

Banded Cube 65

Banded Octahedron

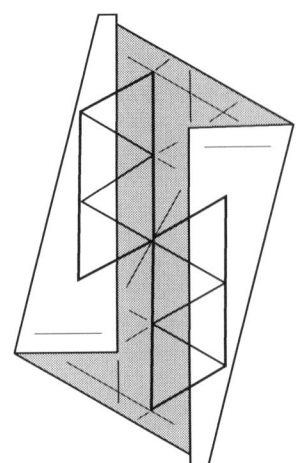

The layout shows two bands of four triangles each. This layout forms an octahedron. Odd symmetry is used.

1. Fold and unfold.

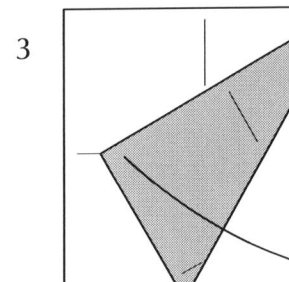

2. Fold at the bottom.

3. Unfold and rotate 180°.

4. Repeat steps 2–3.

5.

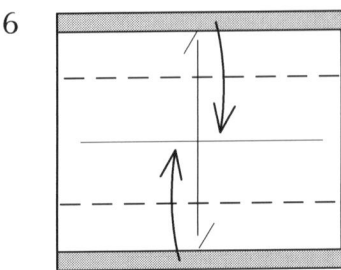

6.

66 *3D Origami Platonic Solids & More*

7

Unfold.

8

Fold and unfold.

9

10

Unfold.

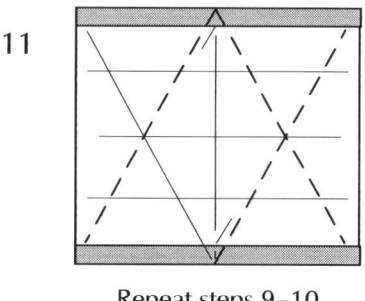

11

Repeat steps 9–10 three more times.

12

13

14

Unfold.

15

Fold and unfold.

16

Unfold.

17

Fold and unfold.

18

Fold the edges to the crease marks.

Banded Octahedron

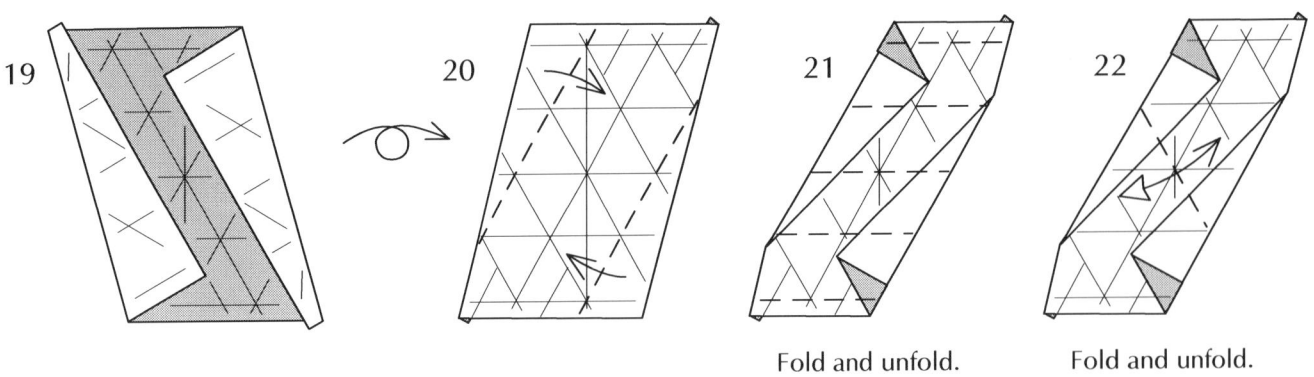

21. Fold and unfold.
22. Fold and unfold.

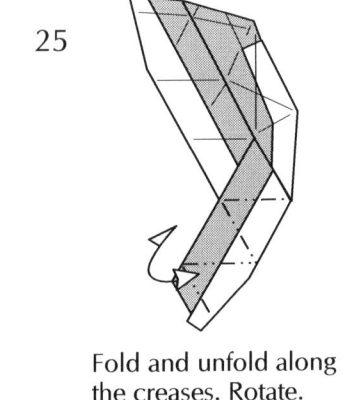

23. Fold and unfold.
24. Puff out at the dot.
25. Fold and unfold along the creases. Rotate.

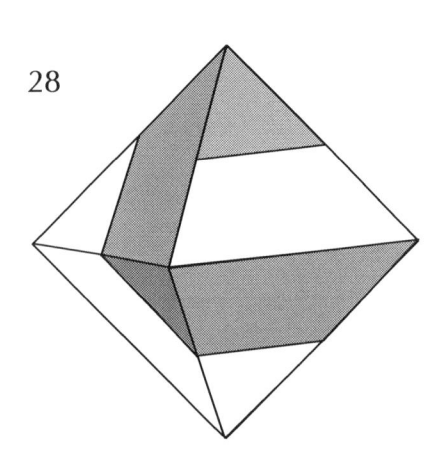

26. Repeat steps 24–25.
27. Tuck inside. The dots will meet.

Banded Octahedron

68   3D Origami Platonic Solids & More

Dimpled Polyhedra

These polyhedra are dimpled versions of some of the Archimedean solids. Archimedean solids are convex polyhedra where the faces are from two or more types of regular polygons and have identical vertices.

Octahemioctahedron

Cubehemioctahedron

Dimpled Rhombicuboctahedron

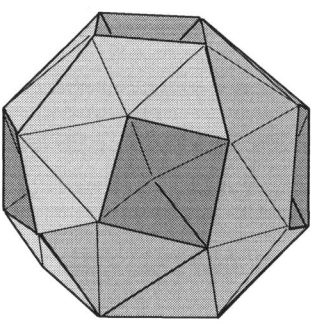

Dimpled Snub Cube

Dimpled Rhombicuboctahedron

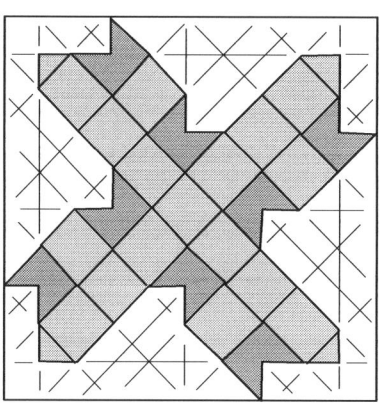

The rhombicuboctahedron has 18 square faces and 8 triagular faces. The dark regions of the crease pattern show the sunken sides. The paper is divided into tenths. Square symmetry is used.

Dimpled Rhombicuboctahedron

13

Fold and unfold.

14

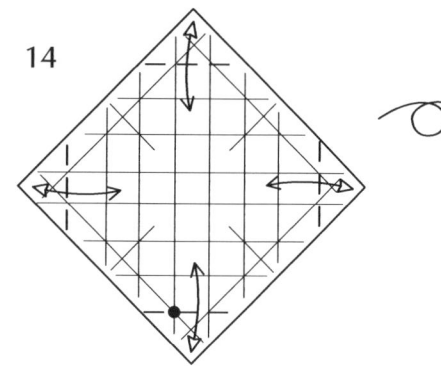

Fold and unfold four times.

15

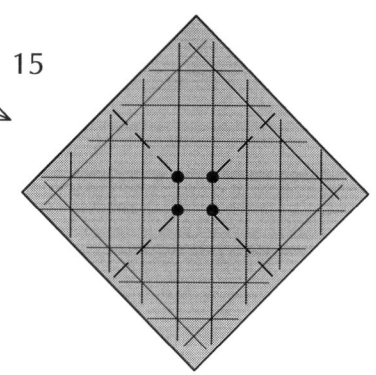

Fold and unfold, extending the creases.

16

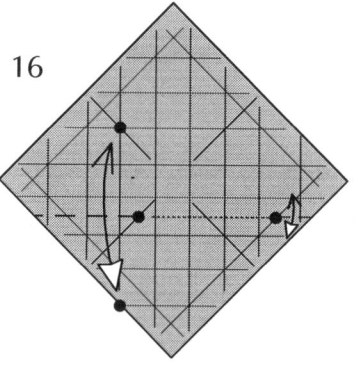

Fold and unfold on the left and a little on the right. Rotate 90°.

17

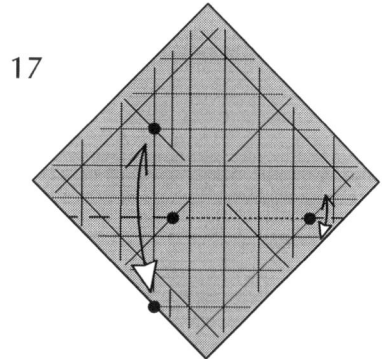

Repeat step 16 three more times. Rotate.

18

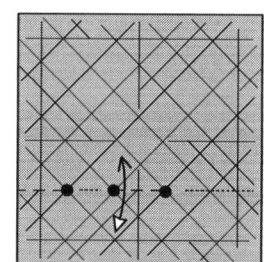

Fold and unfold on the left and in the middle. Rotate 90°.

19

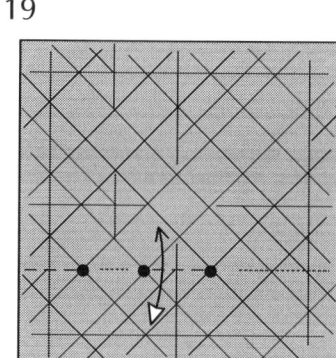

Repeat step 18 three more times.

20

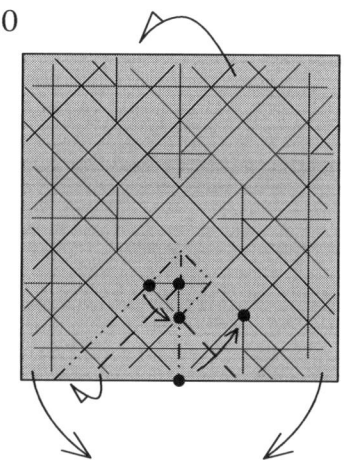

Push in at the upper center dot to form a sunken triangle. The other pairs of dots meet.

21

22

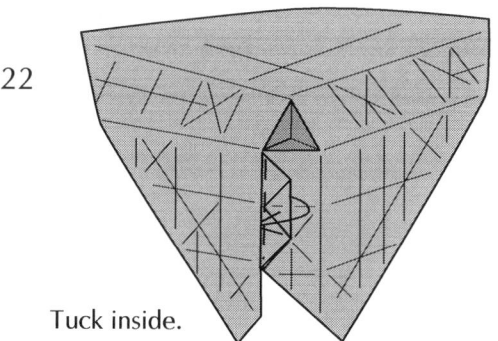

Tuck inside.

Dimpled Rhombicuboctahedron 71

Cubehemioctahedron

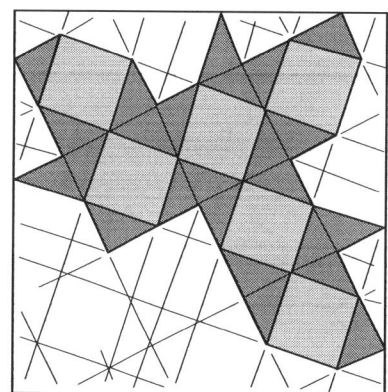

The cubehemioctahedron can be formed from a cube with sunken corners. This model uses 3/4 square symmetry. The darker paper in the crease pattern shows the sunken sides.

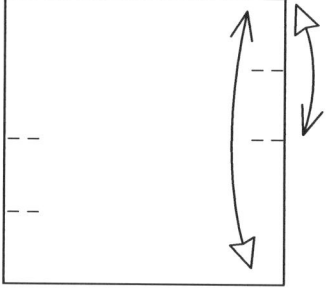

1. Make small marks by folding and unfolding in quarters.

2. Fold and unfold.

3. Fold and unfold.

4.

5.

6. Unfold.

Cubehemioctahedron 73

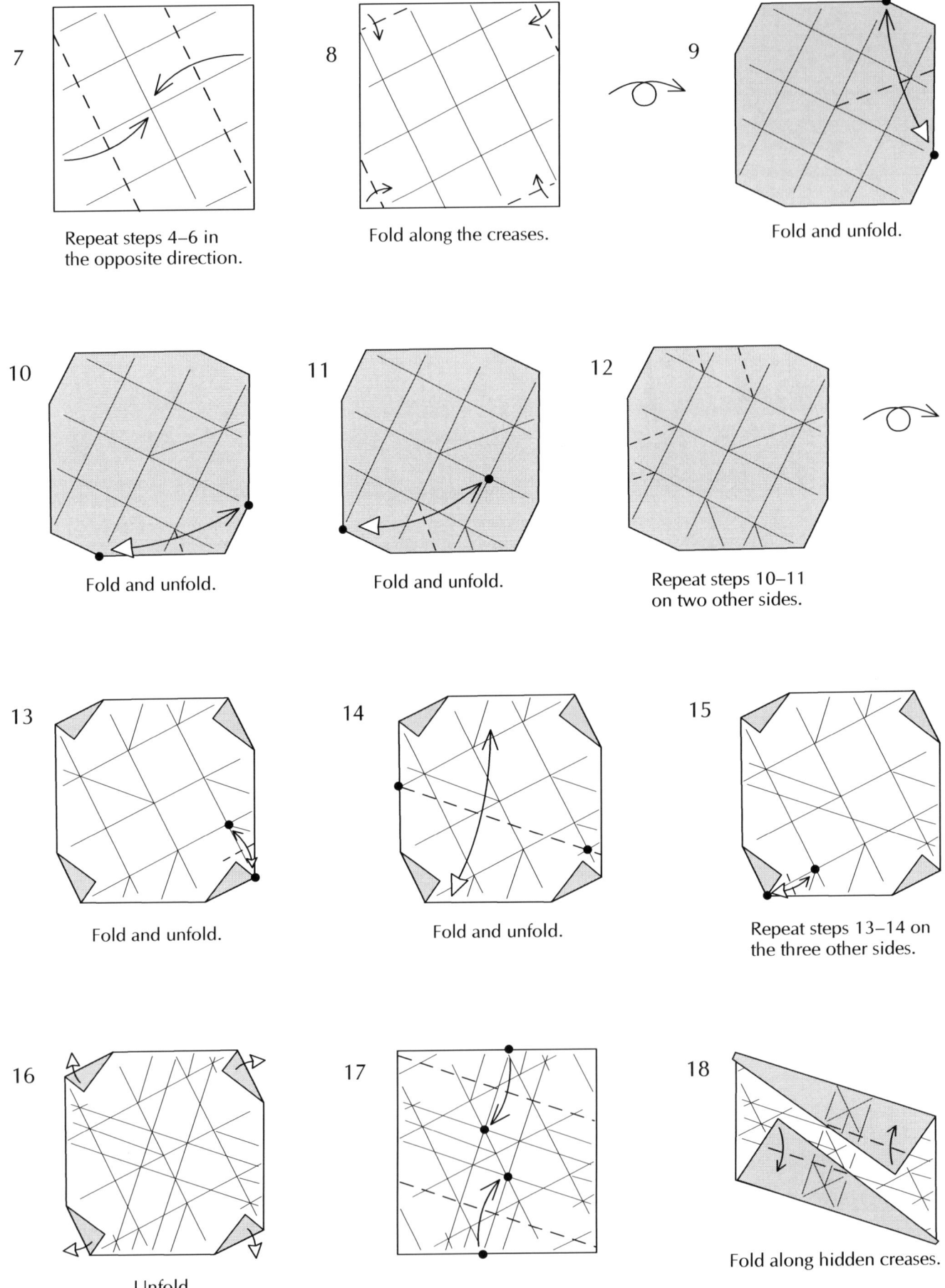

74   *3D Origami Platonic Solids & More*

19. Unfold.

20. Repeat steps 17–19 on the other sides.

21. Fold and unfold along the creases.

22. Turn over and rotate the dot to the bottom.

23. Push in at the center to form a sunken triangle. The pairs of dots meet.

24. Push in at the upper dot to form a sunken triangle.

25. Fold both layers together.

26. Rotate so the corner with the dot shows at the front left.

27. Push in at the dot to form a sunken triangle.

28. Tuck inside.

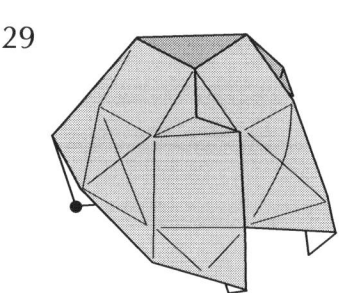

29. Repeat steps 27–28 on the corner with the dot.

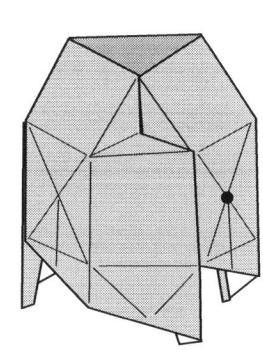

30. Rotate the dot to the center.

Cubehemioctahedron

31

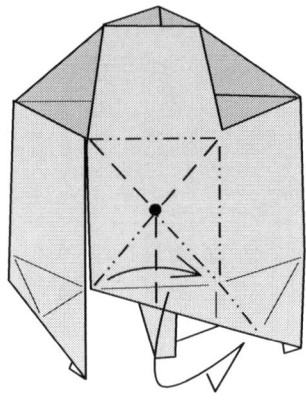

Push in at the dot to form a sunken triangle.

32

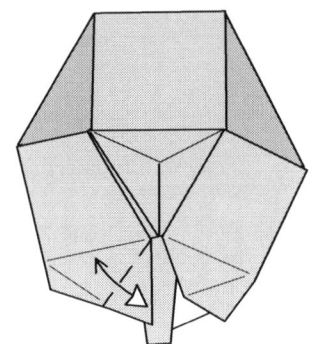

Fold and unfold along the crease.

33

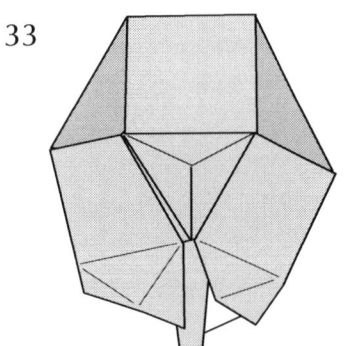

Repeat steps 31–32 two more times going around.

34

Begin to form the bottom sunken triangle by folding toward the inside center and tucking.

35

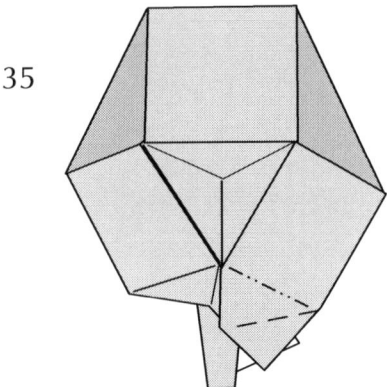

Repeat step 34 two more times to complete the bottom sunken triangle.

36

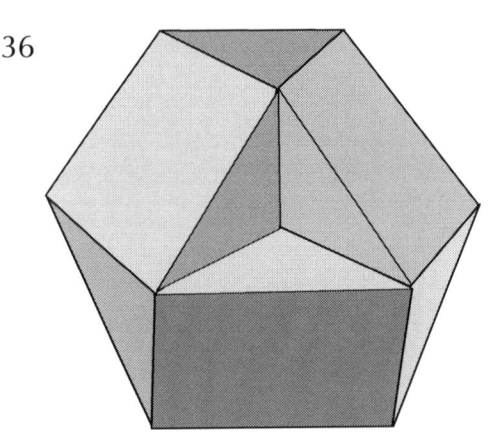

Cubehemioctahedron

76   *3D Origami Platonic Solids & More*

Octahemioctahedron

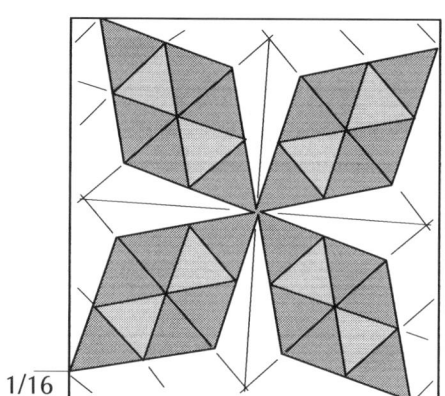

The octahemioctahedron can be formed from an octahedron with sunken vertices. The structure is similar to that of Octahedron (2) but the tab is 1/16 instead of 1/8. This makes for a larger model. The darker regions represent the sunken sides.

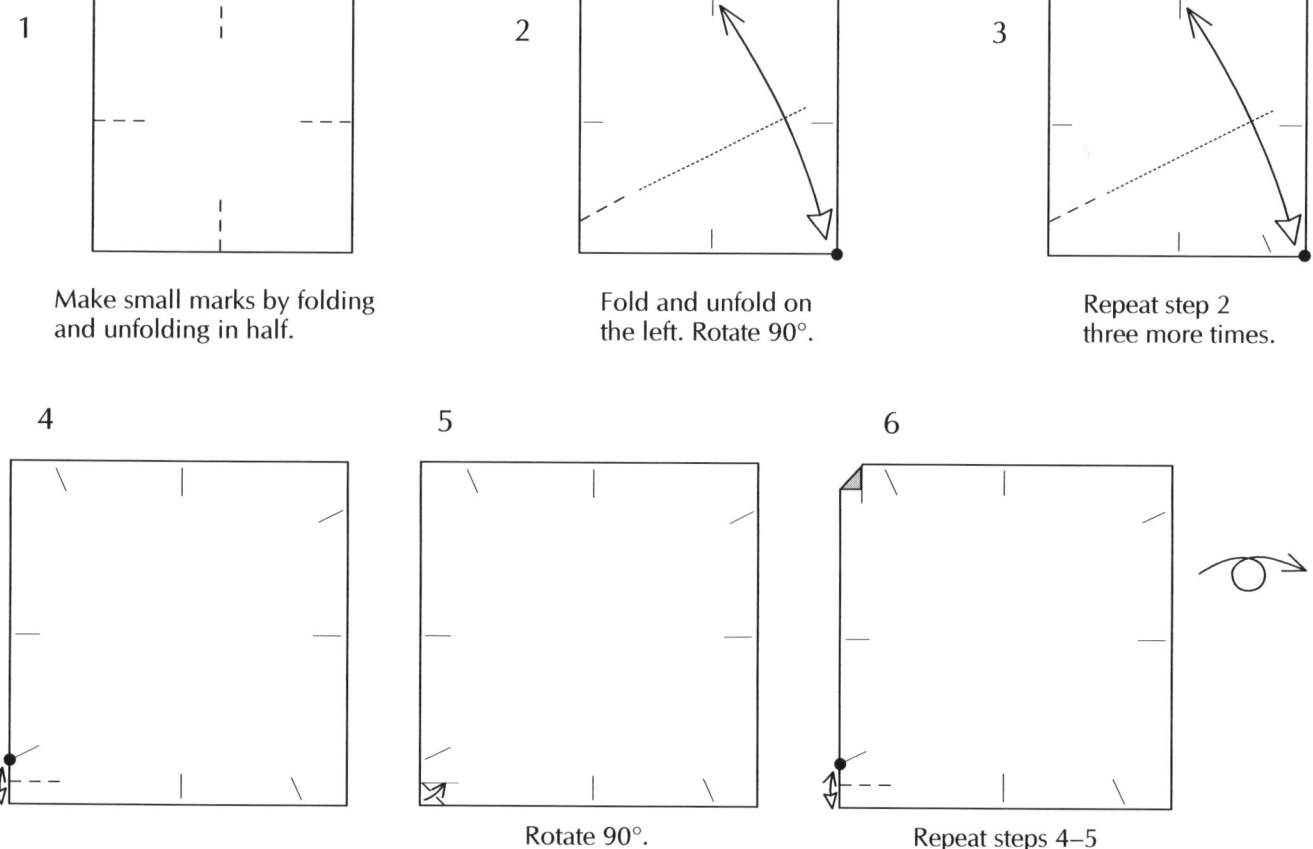

1. Make small marks by folding and unfolding in half.
2. Fold and unfold on the left. Rotate 90°.
3. Repeat step 2 three more times.
4.
5. Rotate 90°.
6. Repeat steps 4–5 three more times.

Octahemioctahedron 77

7

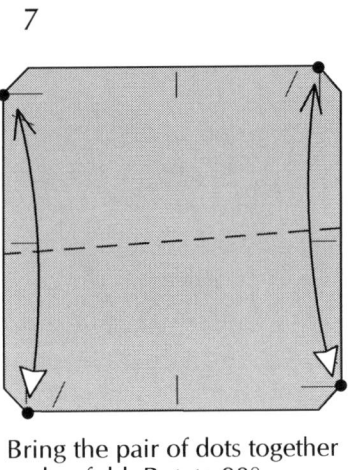

Bring the pair of dots together and unfold. Rotate 90°.

8

Fold and unfold.

9

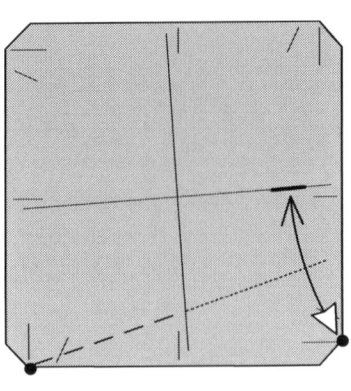

Fold and unfold on the left. Rotate 90°.

10

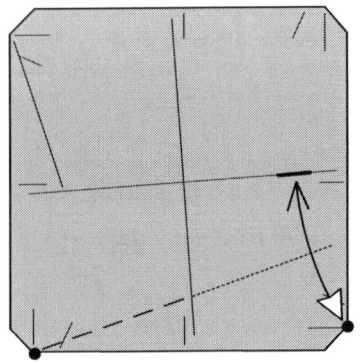

Repeat step 9 three more times.

11

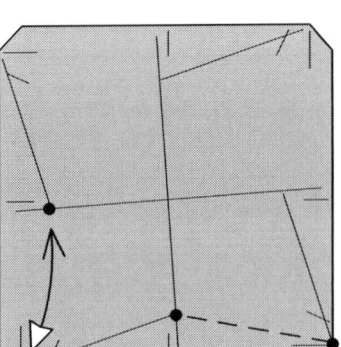

Fold and unfold on the right. Rotate 90°.

12

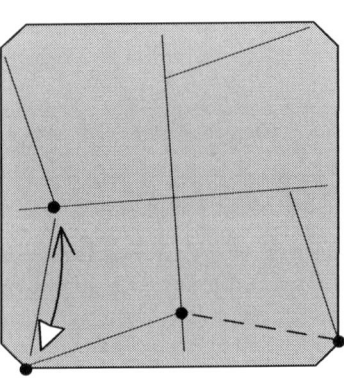

Repeat step 11 three more times.

13

14

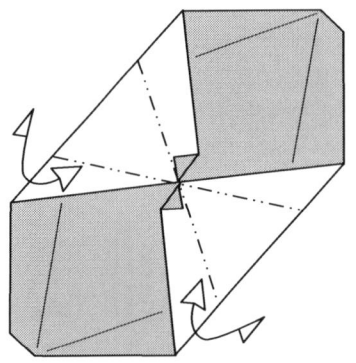

Fold and unfold along the creases.

15

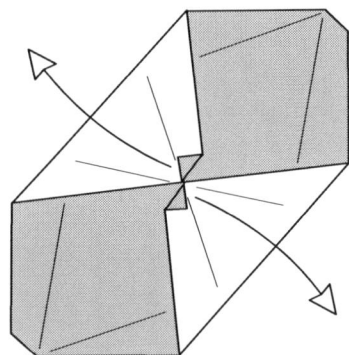

Unfold.

78   3D Origami Platonic Solids & More

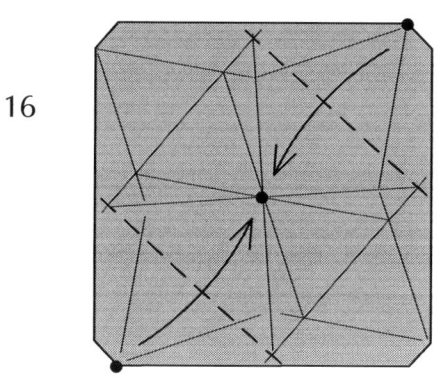

16. Repeat steps 13–15 in the other direction.

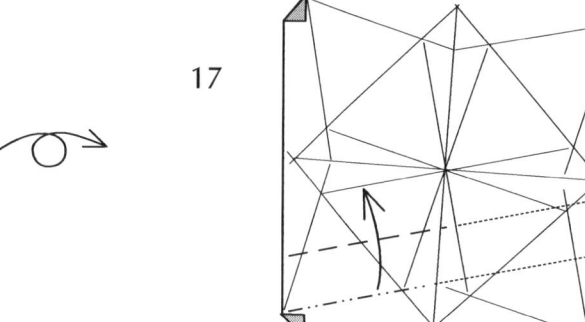

17. Fold to the crease line. Only crease on the left.

18. Unfold.

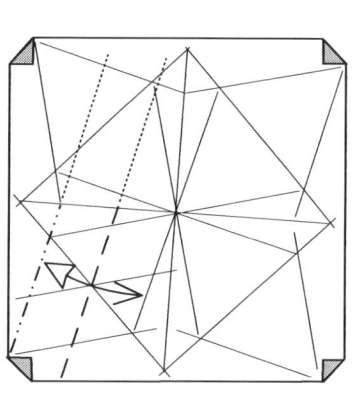

19. Fold to the crease line and unfold. Only crease on the bottom. Rotate 90°.

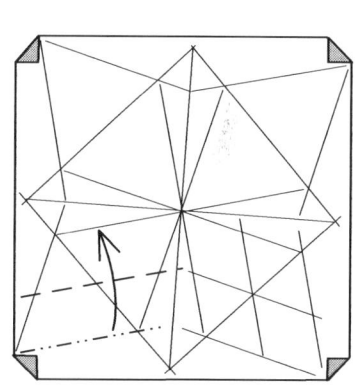

20. Repeat steps 17–19 three more times. Rotate.

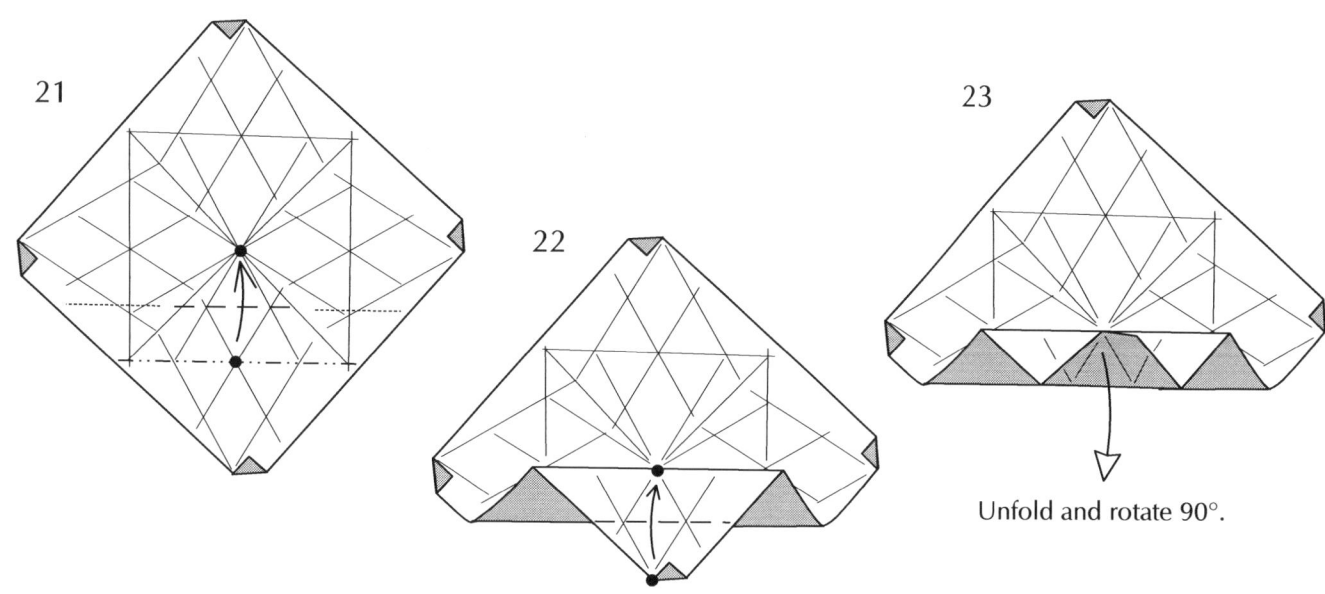

23. Unfold and rotate 90°.

Octahemioctahedron 79

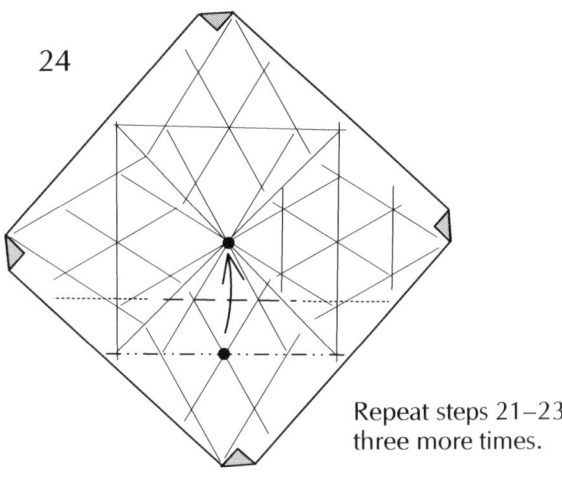

24

Repeat steps 21–23 three more times.

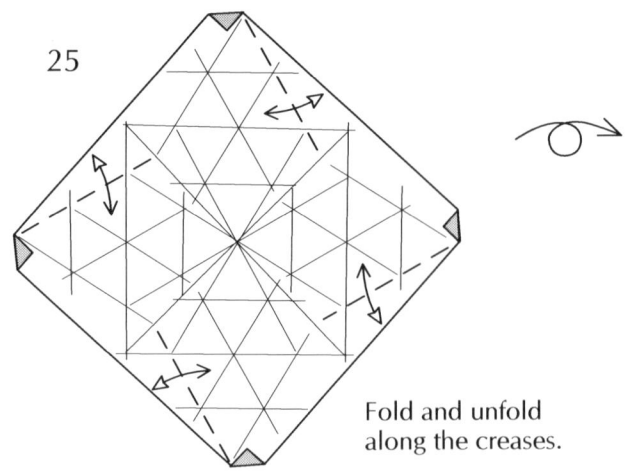

25

Fold and unfold along the creases.

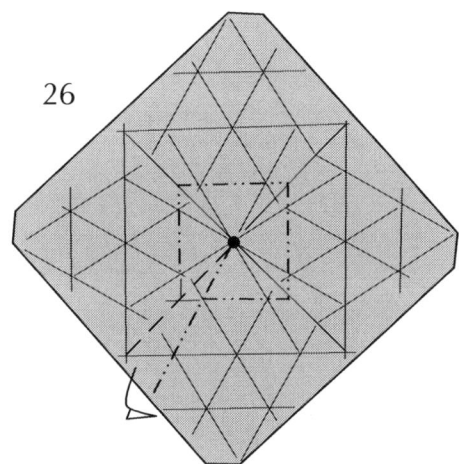

26

Push in at the dot.

27

Repeat step 26 three more times to form a sunken square.

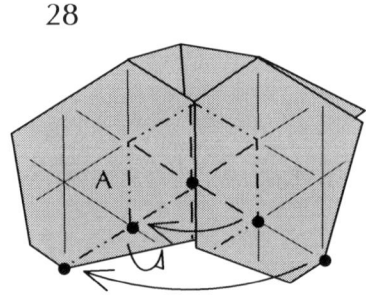

28

Push in at the upper dot to form another sunken square. The other pairs of dots will meet. Flatten inside, especially under triangle A.

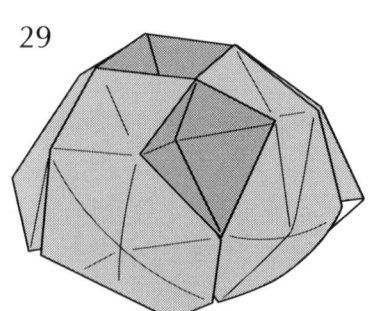

29

Repeat step 28 on the three other sides.

30

The last sunken square is formed by four connected reverse folds.

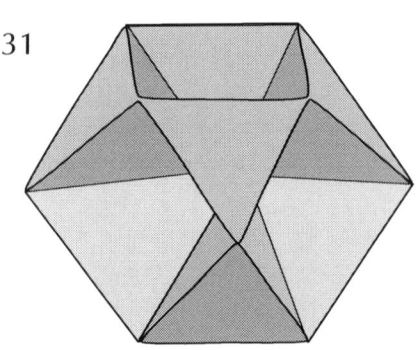

31

Octahemioctahedron

80　*3D Origami Platonic Solids & More*

Dimpled Snub Cube

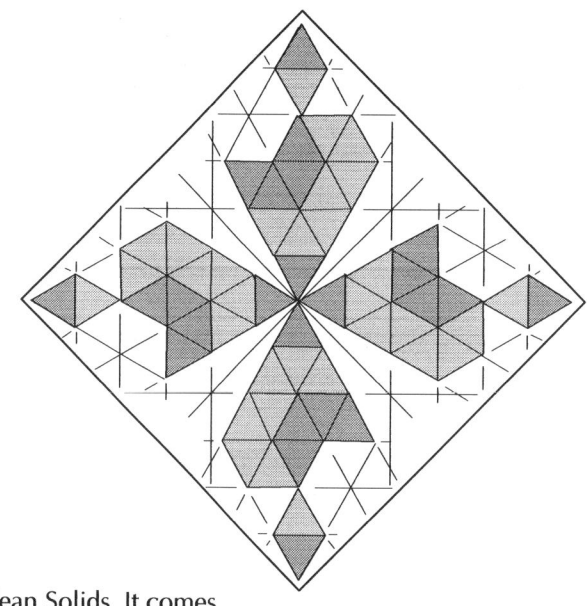

The snub cube is one of thirteen Archimedean Solids. It comes in a left and right handed form. This polyhedron has six dimpled square sides and 32 equilateral triangles. Square symmetry is used. The darker areas refer to the sunken squares.

1.
Fold and unfold.

2.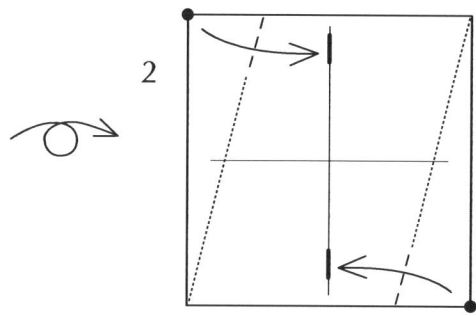
Bring the corners to the lines. Crease at the top and bottom.

3.
Unfold.

4.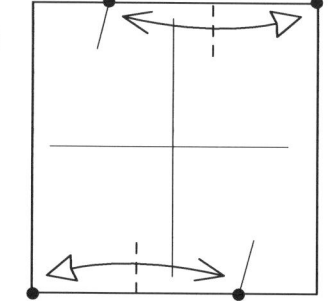
Fold and unfold at the top and bottom.

5.

6.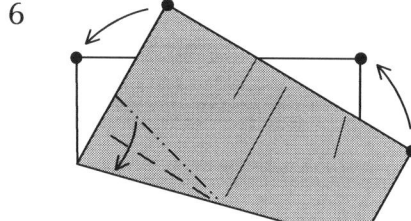
Valley-fold along the crease. Turn over and repeat.

Dimpled Snub Cube 81

Dimpled Snub Cube 83

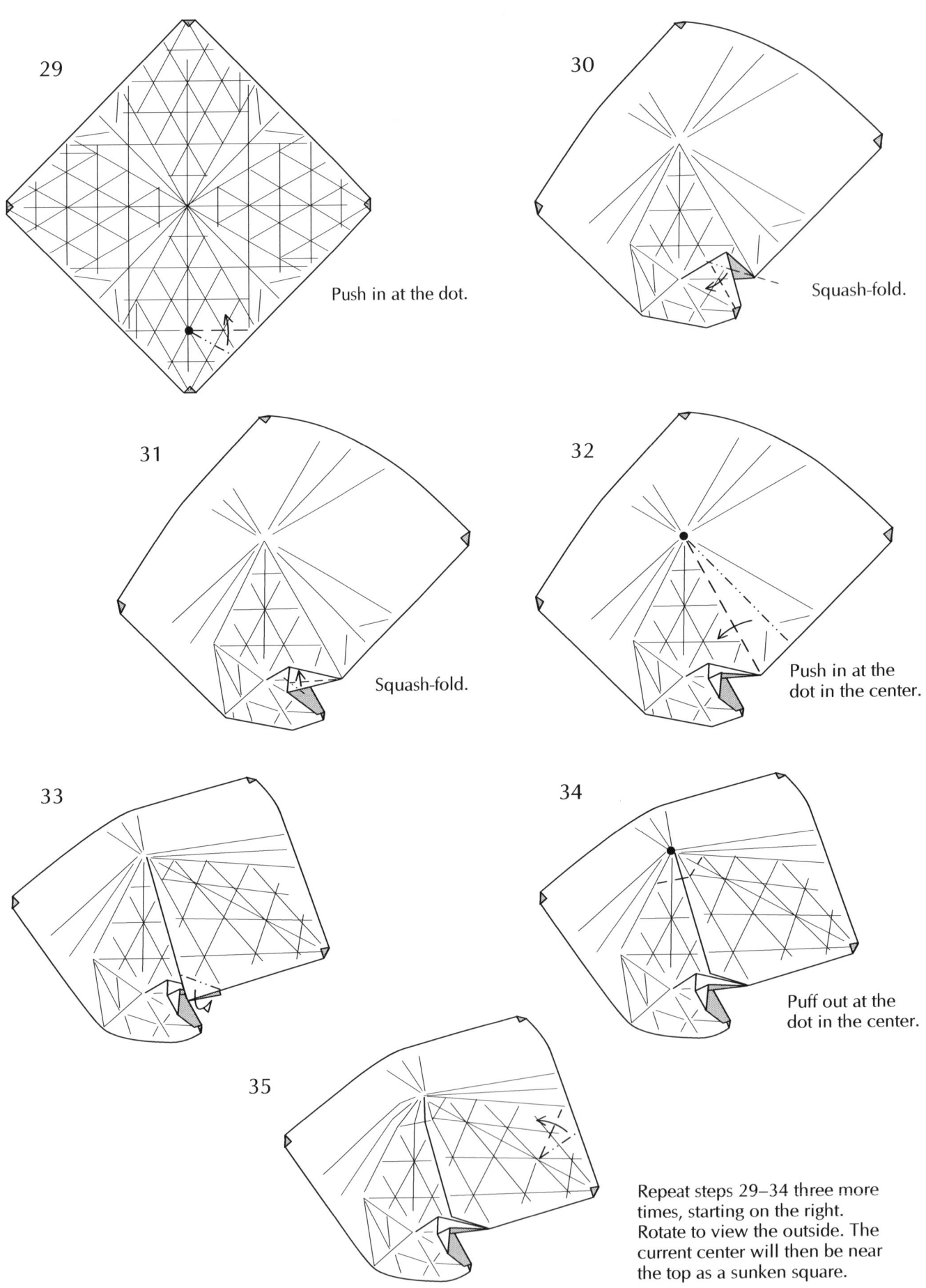

29. Push in at the dot.

30. Squash-fold.

31. Squash-fold.

32. Push in at the dot in the center.

33.

34. Puff out at the dot in the center.

35. Repeat steps 29–34 three more times, starting on the right. Rotate to view the outside. The current center will then be near the top as a sunken square.

84 3D Origami Platonic Solids & More

36

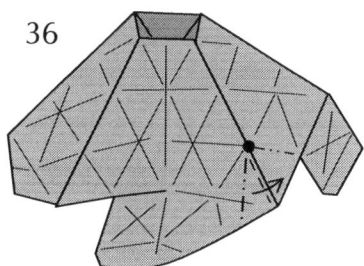

Puff out at the dot.

37

Unfold.

38

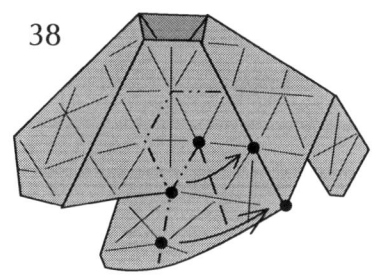

Push in at the upper dot to form a sunken square.

39

Repeat step 36 on the hidden layers so triangle A will cover triangle B.

40

Fold and unfold.

41

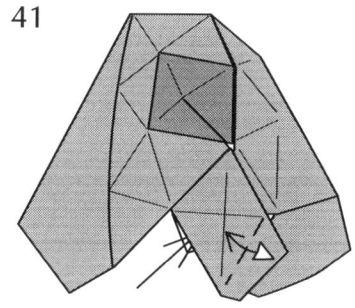

Fold and unfold. Note the pocket.

42

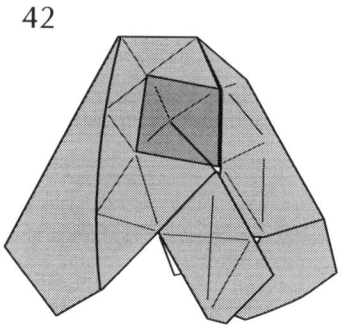

Repeat steps 36–41 three more times.

43

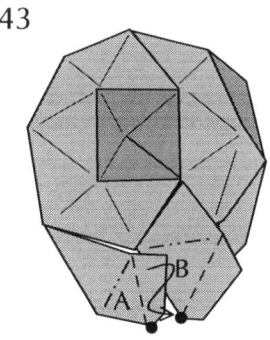

Triangles A and B are two of the four that will form the bottom sunken square. Tuck each of the flaps inside the pockets to close the model.

44

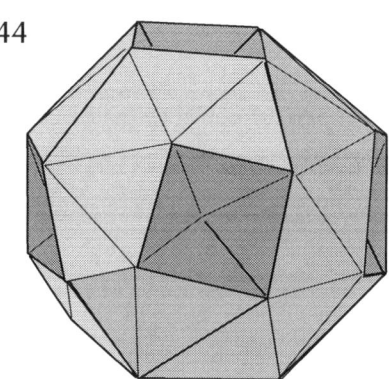

Dimpled Snub Cube

Octahedra

Octahedra are polyhedra with eight faces. This collection includes a dipyramid, trapezohedron, prism, and antiprism.

Dipyramids, or diamonds, are composed of a pair of identical pyramids joined at the base. All the faces are triangles.

A trapezohedron, or antidiamond, is composed of congruent kites where three angles are identical. All the faces are symmetrically staggered.

A prism is a polyhedron where two congruent polygons are connected by parallelograms.

An antiprism is a polyhedron where two congruent polygons are connected by a band of alternating triangles.

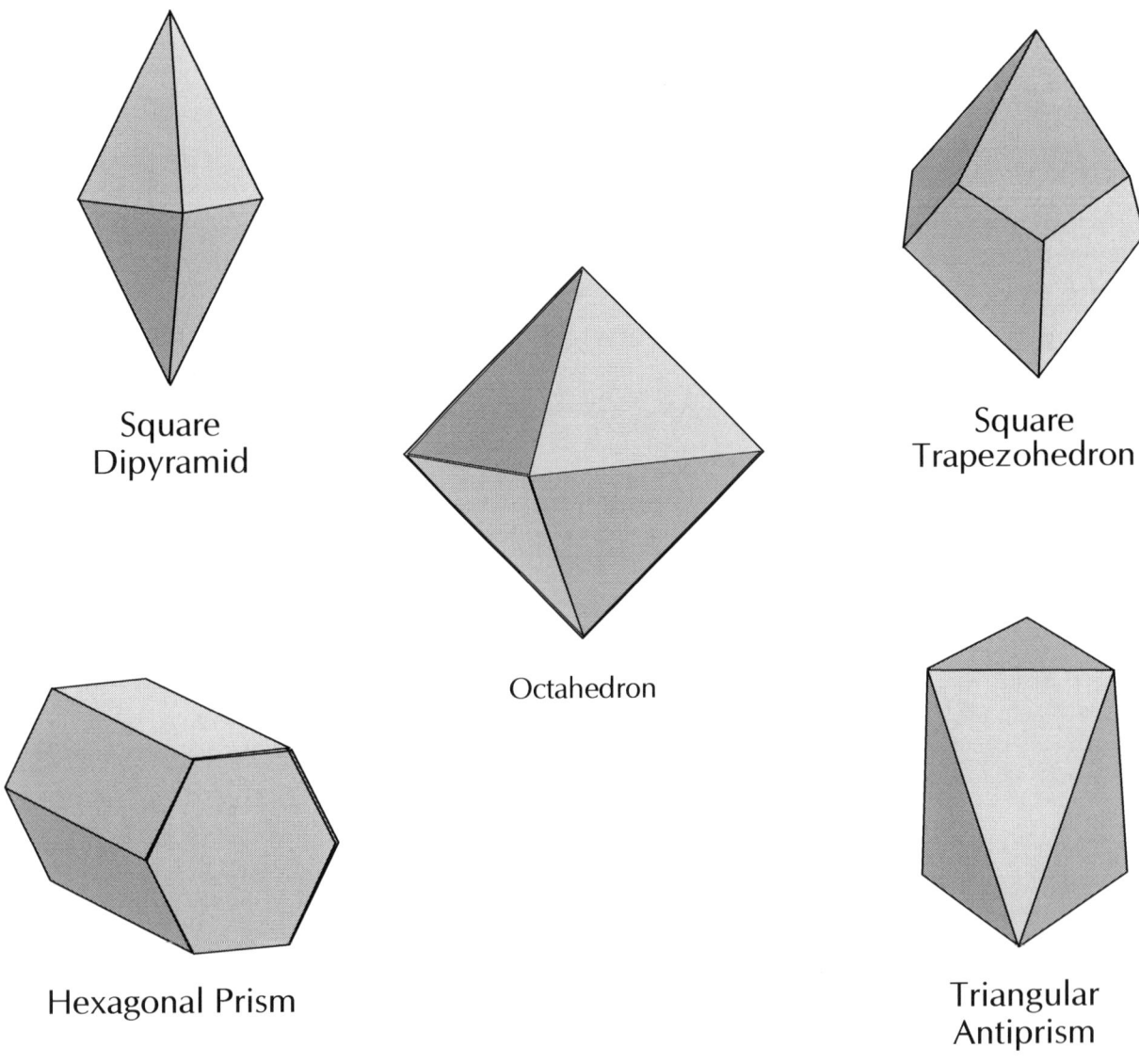

Square Dipyramid

Square Trapezohedron

Octahedron

Hexagonal Prism

Triangular Antiprism

86   *3D Origami Platonic Solids & More*

Square Dipyramid

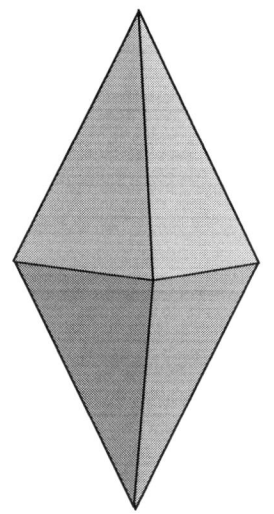

A square dipyramid is composed of eight identical isosceles triangles. For this model, the angles of each face are 36°, 72°, and 72°. Odd symmetry is used.

1.
Fold and unfold.

2.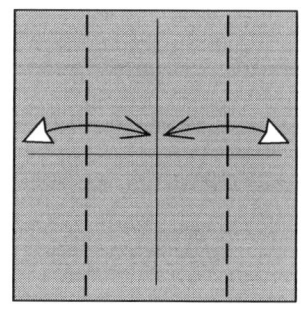
Fold and unfold in the center and on the edges.

3.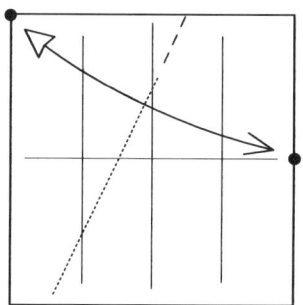
Fold and unfold at the top.

4.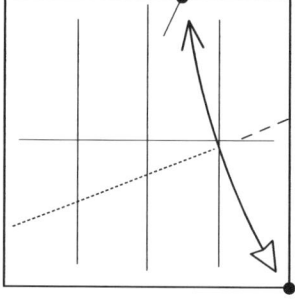
Fold and unfold on the right.

5.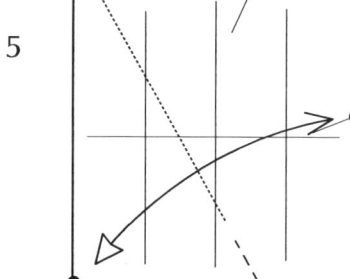
Fold and unfold on the bottom. Rotate 180°.

6.
Repeat steps 3–5.

7.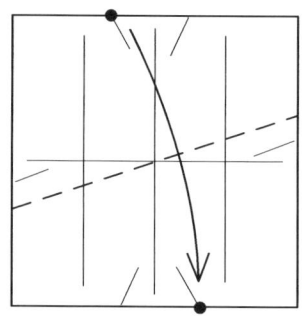

8. Valley-fold along the crease. The dots will meet. Turn over and repeat.

9.
Bisect the angles and repeat behind.

Square Dipyramid 87

Square Trapezodedron

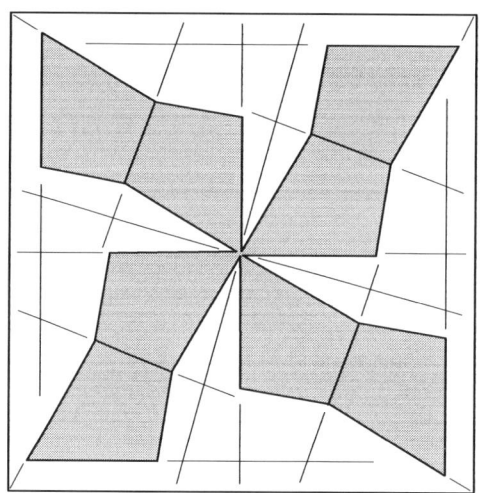

Trapezohedra are beautiful shapes composed of kite-shaped faces staggered symmetrically. Represented through origami, these shapes present challenges to design and fold. The results are stunning.

A square trapezohedron is composed of eight identical kites. For this model, the angles of each face are 60°, 100°, 100°, and 100°. Square symmetry is used.

1

Fold and unfold.

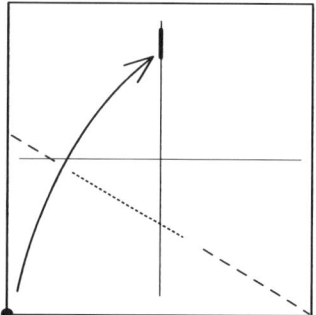

2

Bring the corner to the line.

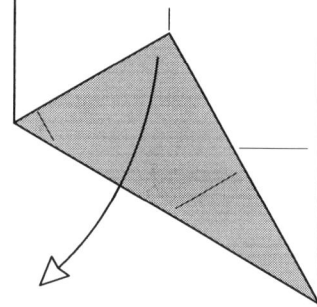

3

Unfold and rotate 180°.

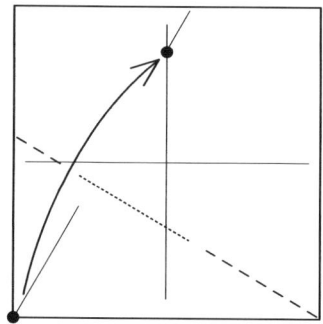

4

Repeat steps 2–3 three more times.

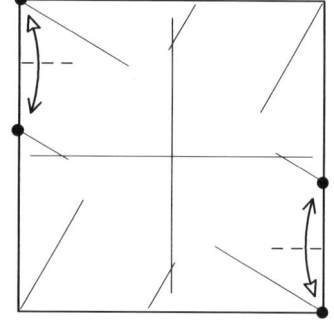

5

Fold and unfold on the edges.

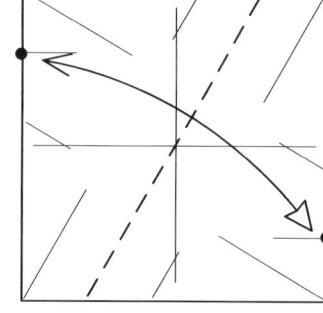

6

Fold and unfold.

Square Trapezohedron 89

7

Fold and unfold.

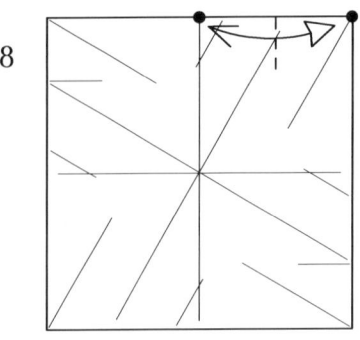

8

Fold and unfold at the top.

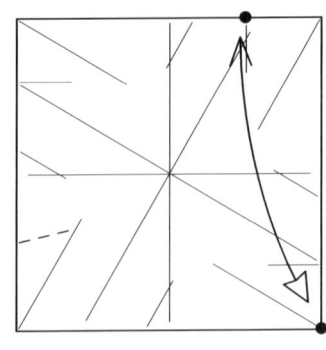

9

Fold and unfold on the left.

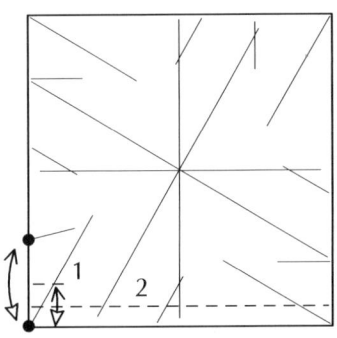

10

1. Fold and unfold on the left.
2. Fold and unfold.
Rotate 90°.

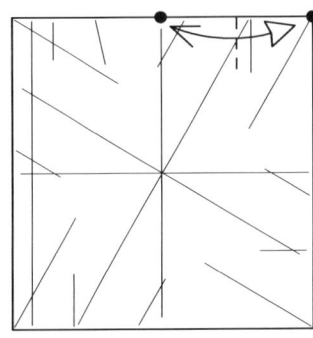

11

Repeat steps 8–10 three more times.

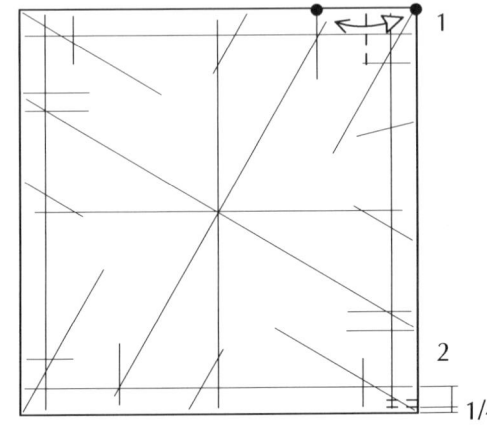

12

1. Fold and unfold at the top.
2. Fold and unfold on the right to find the 1/4 mark of the thin strip near the bottom.

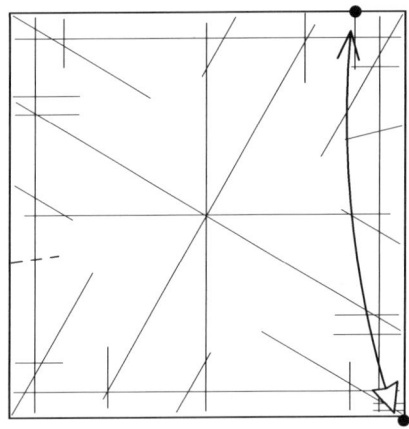

13

Bring the bottom right corner to the landmark at the top. Fold and unfold on the left.

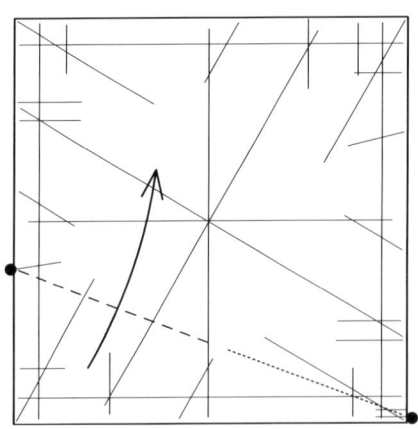

14

Fold along a line from the landmark on the left to the 1/4 landmark on the right. Crease on the left side.

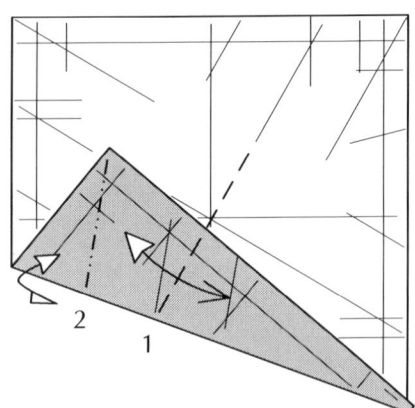

15

Fold and unfold both layers.
1. Valley-fold along a hidden crease.
2. Mountain-fold along the crease.

90   3D Origami Platonic Solids & More

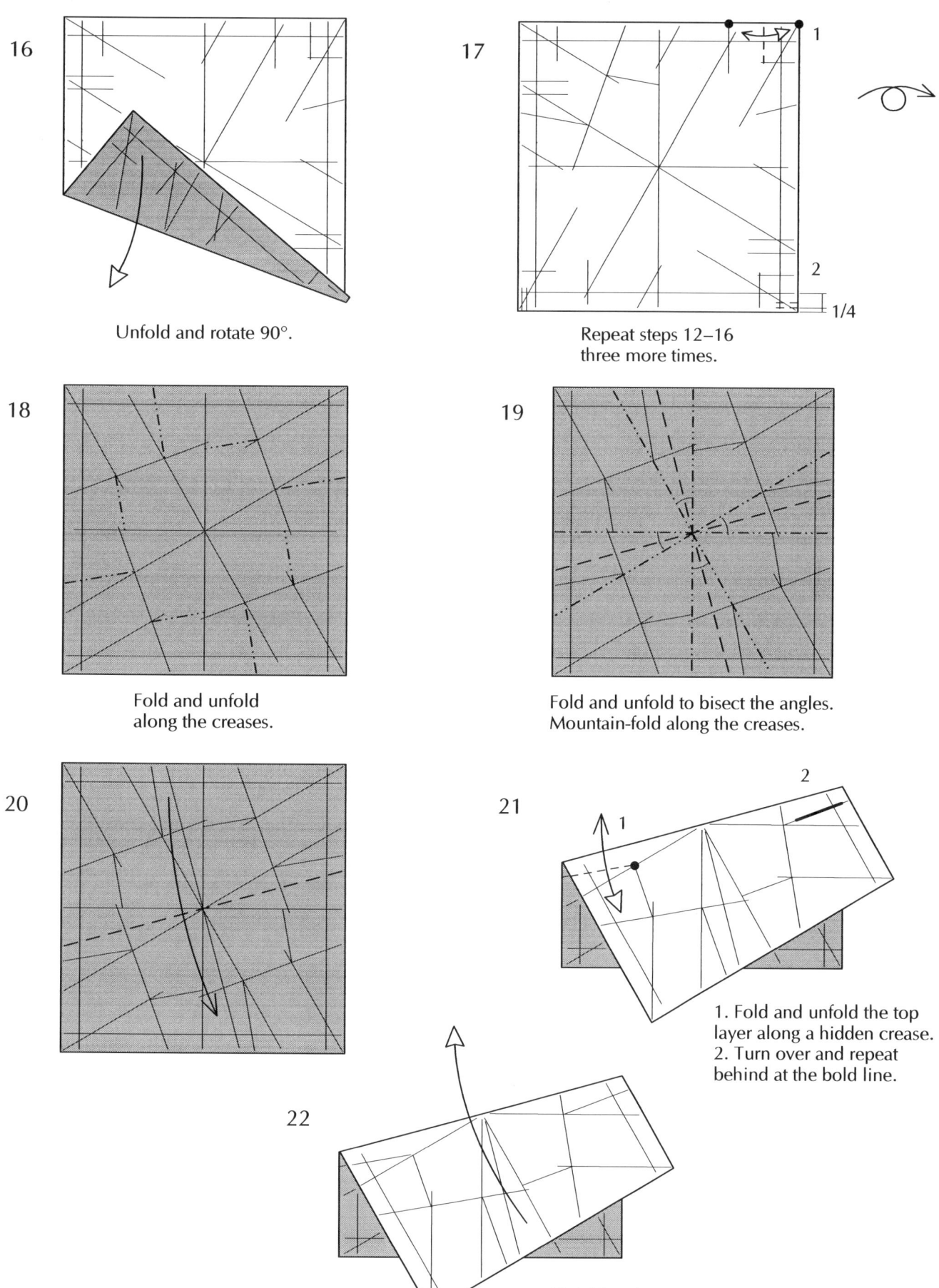

16. Unfold and rotate 90°.

17. Repeat steps 12–16 three more times.

18. Fold and unfold along the creases.

19. Fold and unfold to bisect the angles. Mountain-fold along the creases.

21.
1. Fold and unfold the top layer along a hidden crease.
2. Turn over and repeat behind at the bold line.

22. Unfold and rotate 90°.

Square Trapezohedron

23

Repeat steps 20–22.

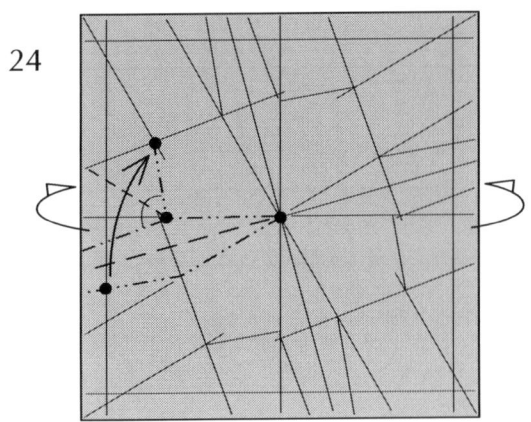

24

The two dots by the left meet, puff out at the other two dots. Rotate.

25

Repeat step 24 three more times.

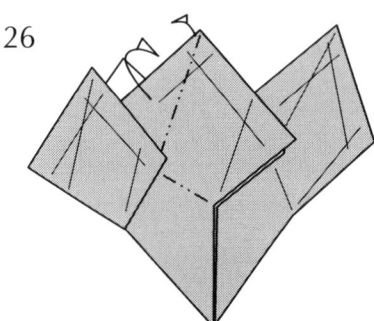

26

Do not flatten completely.

27

28

Fold and unfold.

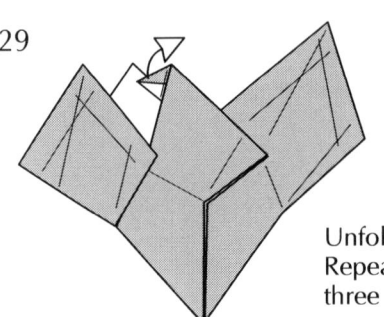

29

Unfold slightly. Repeat steps 26–29 three more times.

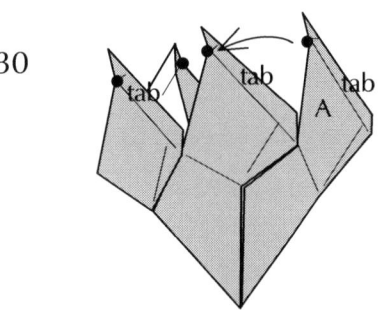

30

Region A will cover the tab. The dots will meet at the top. Repeat all around. The model closes with a four-way twist lock.

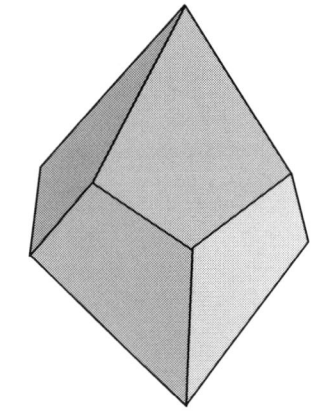

31

Square Trapezohedron

Hexagonal Prism

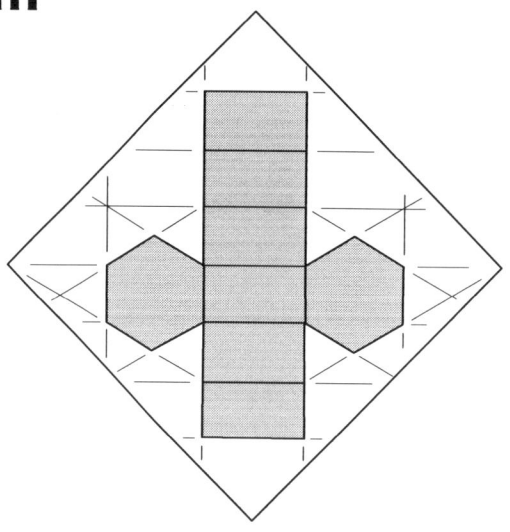

This hexagonal prism is composed of two hexagons and six rectangles. The height of the hexagon is the same as the length of the rectangle. The pair of prisms shown above have the same height.

1.
Fold and unfold.

2.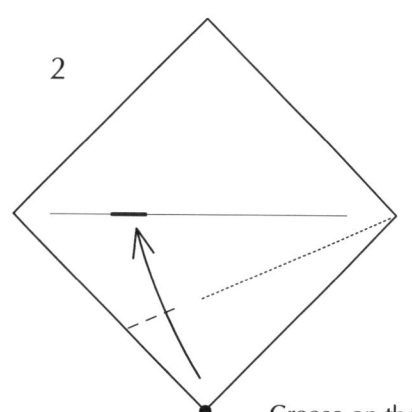
Crease on the left.

3.
Unfold.

4.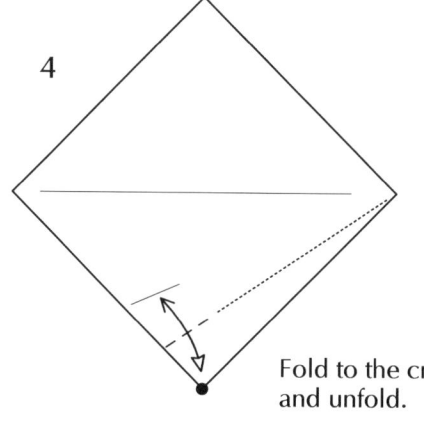
Fold to the crease and unfold.

5.

6.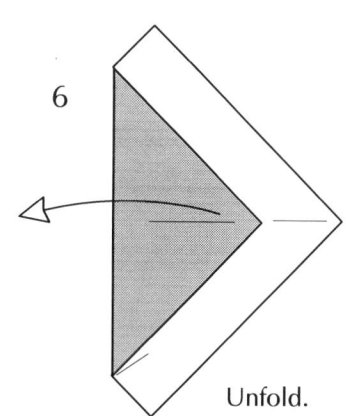
Unfold.

Hexagonal Prism 93

7.

8.

9. Unfold.

10.

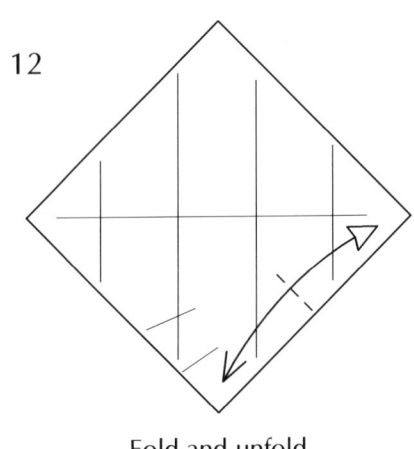

11. Unfold.

12. Fold and unfold on the right.

13. Fold to the line but do not crease between the dots.

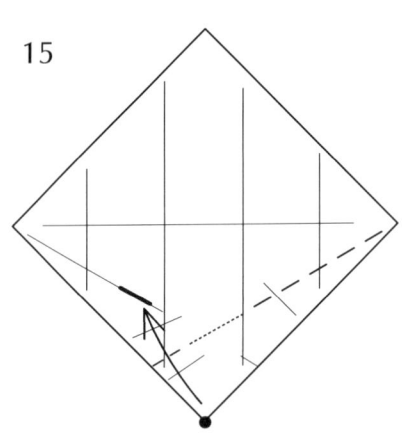

14. Unfold.

15.

94 *3D Origami Platonic Solids & More*

16

17

18

19
Fold behind.

20
Unfold.

21

22

23
Unfold.

24
Fold and unfold.

Fold and unfold.

Fold and unfold.

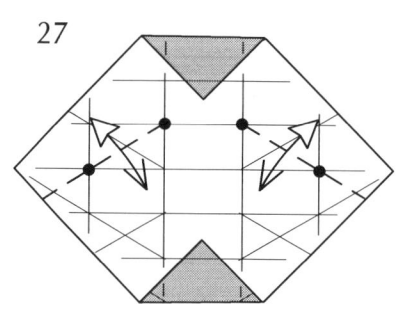

Fold and unfold.

Hexagonal Prism 95

28. Unfold.

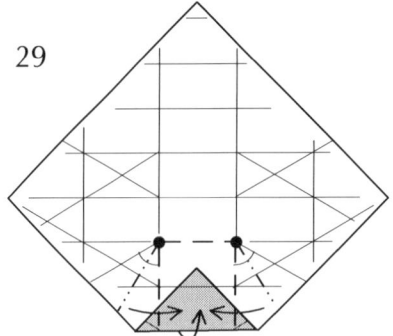

29. Push in at the dots and bisect the angles. Rotate to view the side.

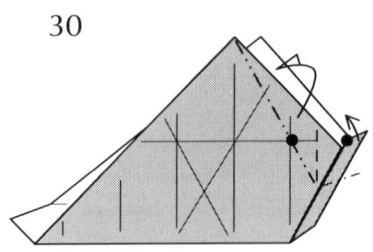

30. The dots will meet. Repeat behind.

31. Repeat behind.

32. Repeat behind.

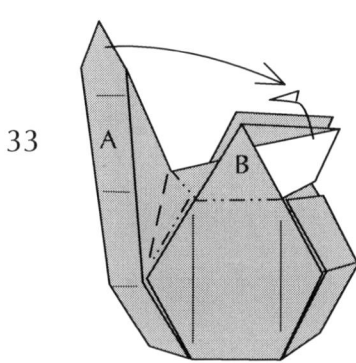

33. Region A will cover B. The dots will meet. Repeat behind.

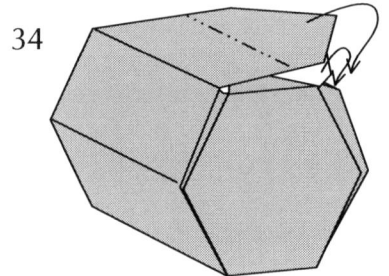

34. Tuck three tabs inside the pocket.

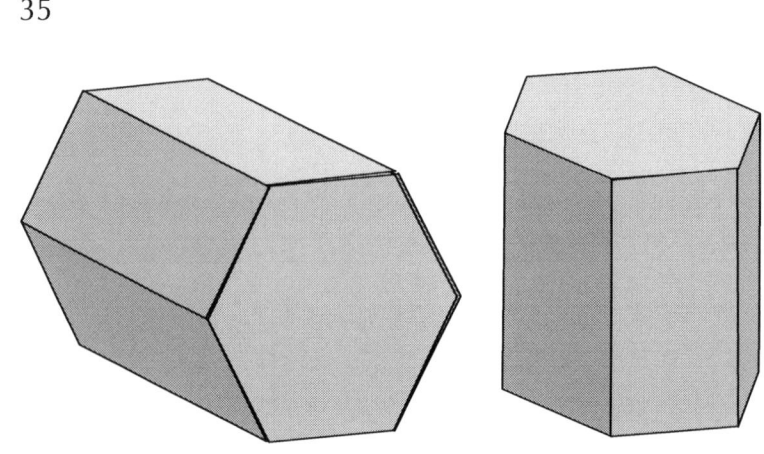

35. Hexagonal Prism

Triangular Antiprism

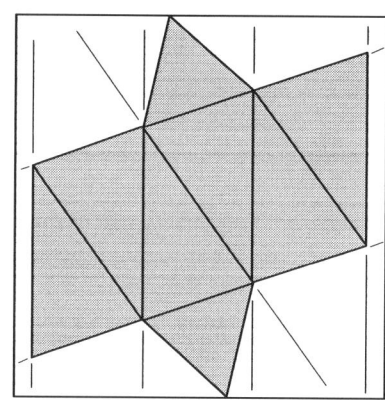

A triangular antiprism is composed of 6 isosceles triangles and two equilateral triangles. In this one, the angles of the isosceles triangles are 36°, 72°, and 72°. The triangles form a band wrapping around.

1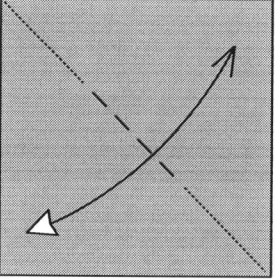

Fold and unfold in the center.

2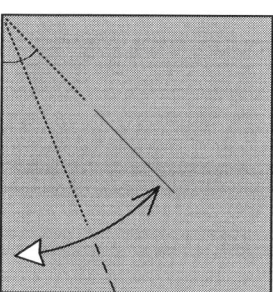

Fold and unfold on the bottom.

3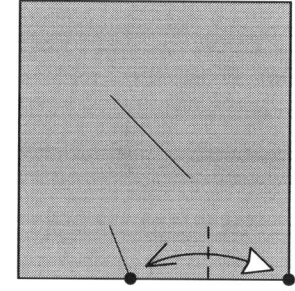

Fold and unfold on the bottom.

4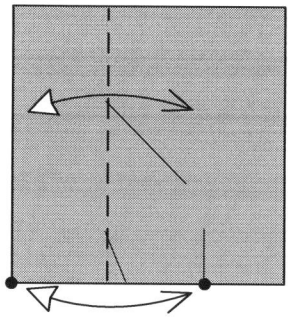

Fold and unfold. Rotate 180°.

5

Repeat steps 2–5.

6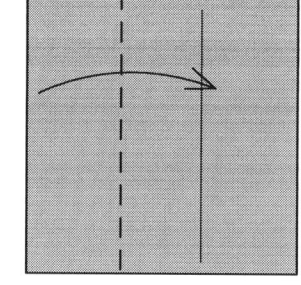

Fold on the crease.

Triangular Antiprism 97

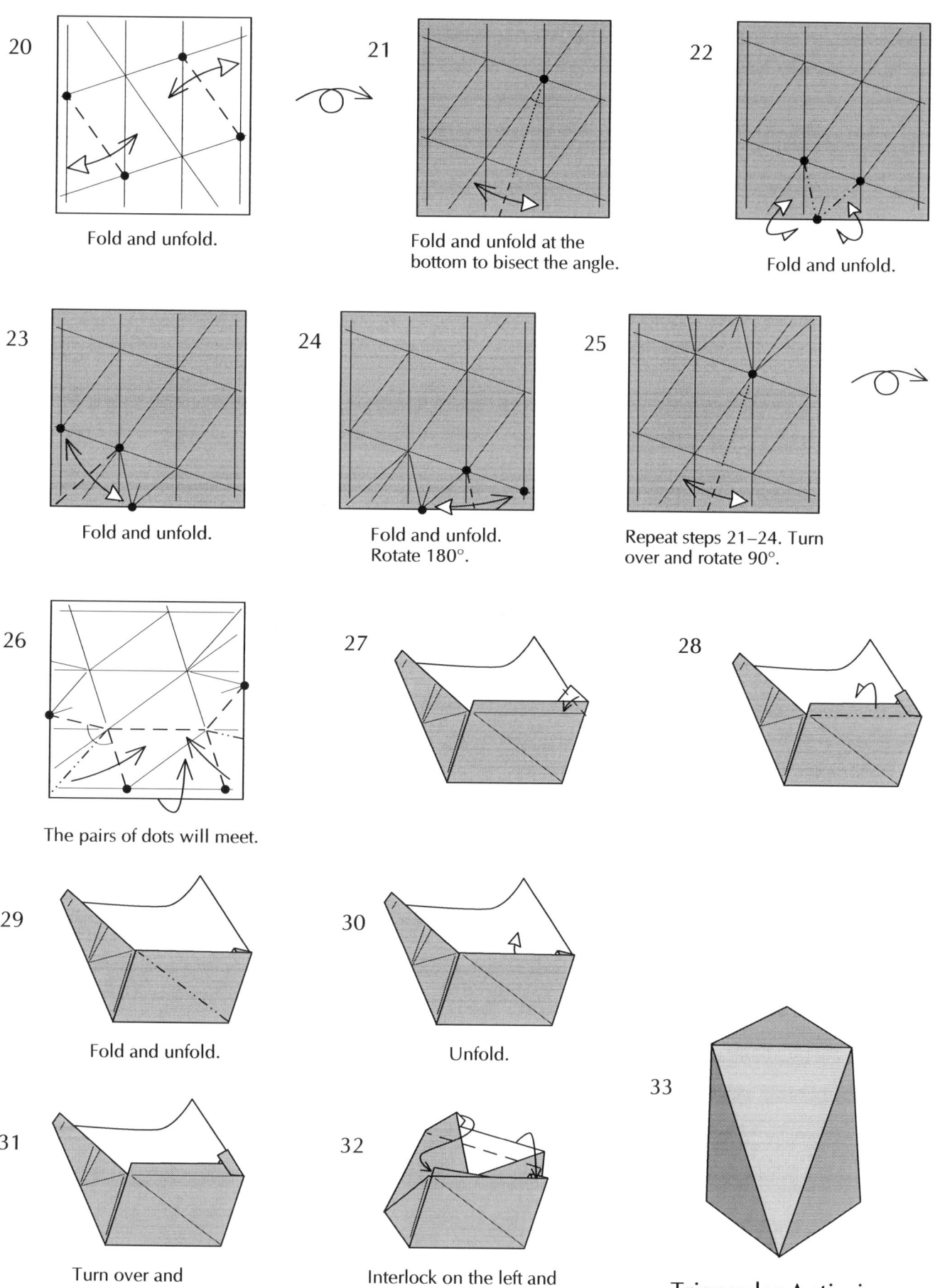

Dodecahedra

Dodecahedra are polyhedra with twelve faces. This collection includes a hexagonal dipyramid, hexagonal trapezohedron, and pentagonal antiprism. The triakis tetrahedron and rhombic dodecahedron are catalan solids whose faces are identical isosceles triangles.

This group highlights the variety of polyhedra that each have twelve faces.

Dodecahedron

Hexagonal Dipyramid

Hexagonal Trapezohedron

Golden Pentagonal Antiprism

Triakis Tetrahedron

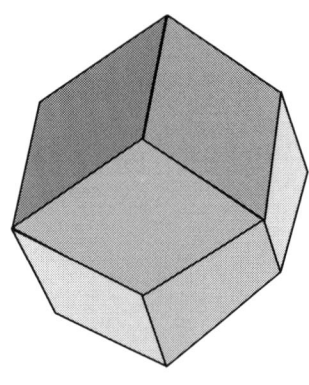

Rhombic Dodecahedron

Hexagonal Dipyramid

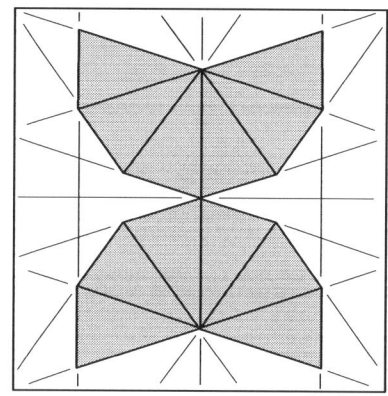

A hexagonal dipyramid has twelve triangular faces. The angles of each triangle are 36°, 72°, and 72°. Odd symmetry is used.

1. Fold and unfold.

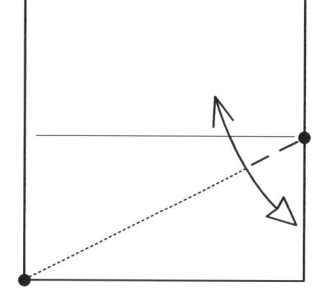

2. Fold and unfold by the right.

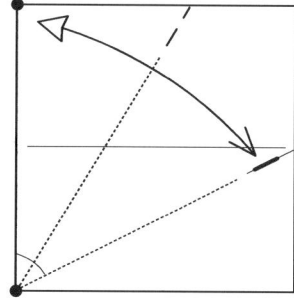

3. Fold and unfold on the top to bisect the angle.

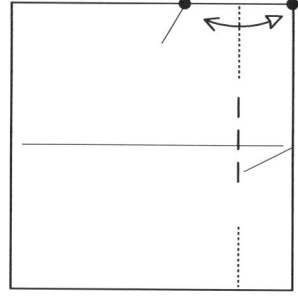

4. Fold and unfold in the center.

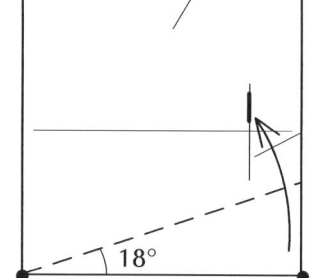

5. Bring the corner to the crease. The 18° angle is exact.

6. Unfold.

Hexagonal Dipyramid

19
Fold and unfold.

20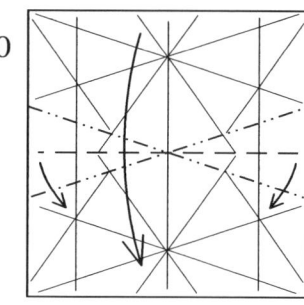
Fold along the creases.

21
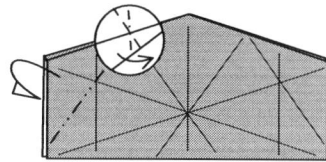
Inside view. Fold the inside layers together for this spine-lock fold. Turn over and repeat.

22
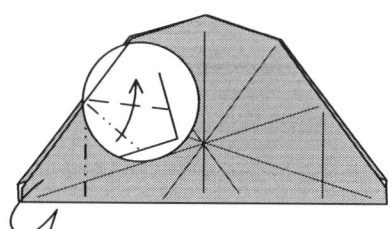
Inside view. Fold the inside layers together for this spine-lock fold. Turn over and repeat.

23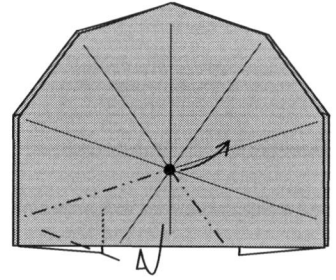
Puff out at the dot and fold along the creases. Turn over and repeat.

24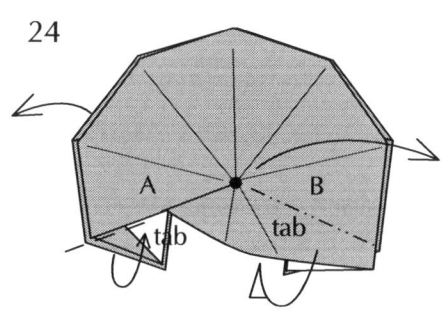
Bring the dot to the right and the one behind to the left. Follow regions A and B into the next step. Fold all the layers of each tab.

25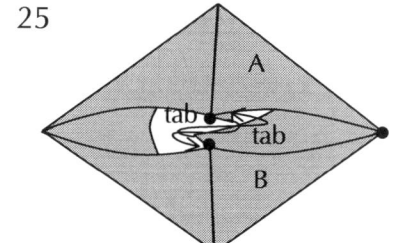
Tuck the two tabs into each other so the center dots meet.

26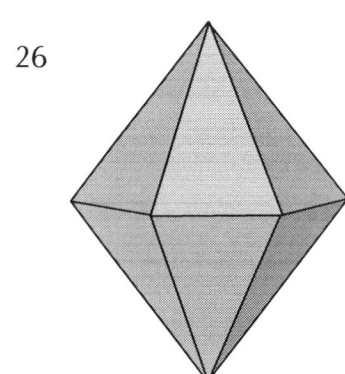

Hexagonal Dipyramid

Hexagonal Dipyramid 103

Hexagonal Trapezohedron

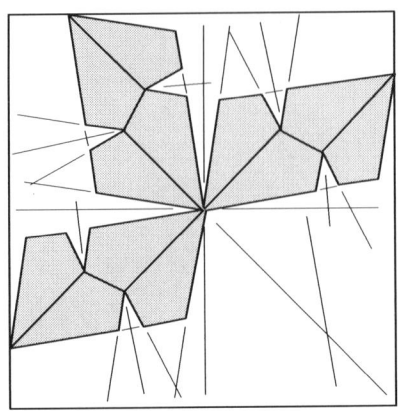

A hexagonal trapezohedron has twelve kites staggered symmetrically. The angles of each of the twelve faces for this trapezodedron are 36°, 108°, 108°, and 108°. The crease pattern shows 3/4 square symmetry.

1. Fold and unfold.

2. Fold and unfold.

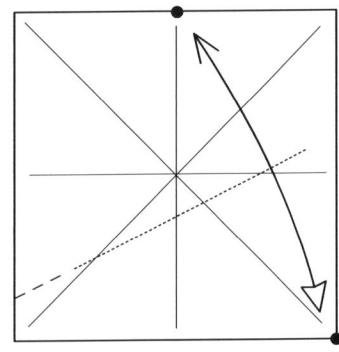

3. Fold and unfold on the left.

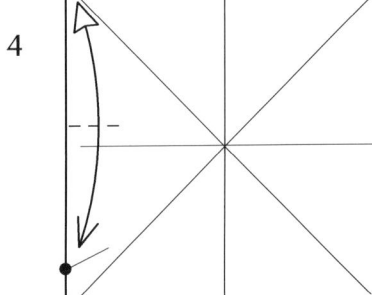

4. Fold and unfold on the left.

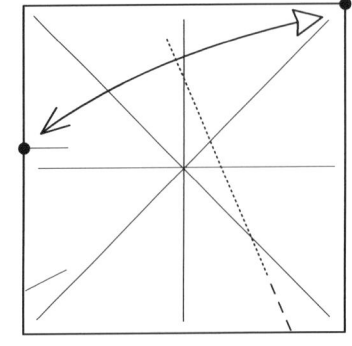

5. Fold and unfold at the bottom.

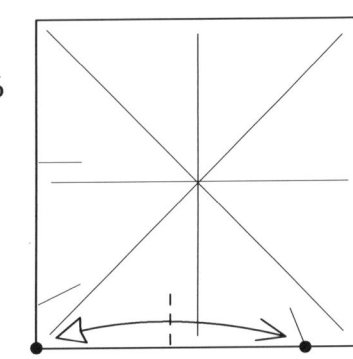

6. Fold and unfold at the bottom. Rotate 180°.

104   *3D Origami Platonic Solids & More*

Hexagonal Trapezohedron 105

30

Reverse-fold.

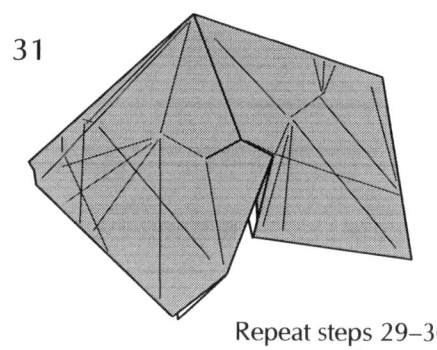

31

Repeat steps 29–30 two more times.

32

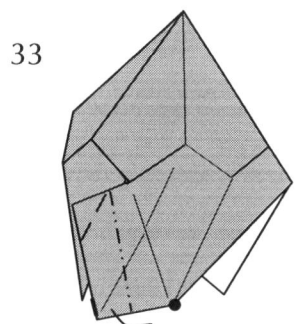

33

Fold the edge to the dot.

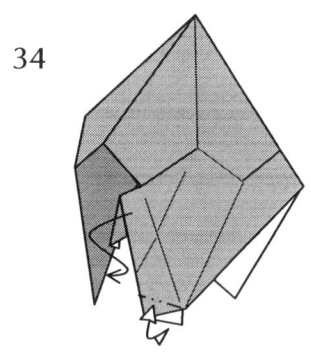

34

Fold and unfold at the bottom. Bring the darker paper to the front.

35

Fold and unfold.

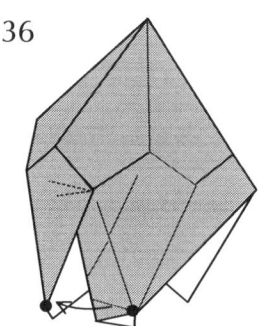

36

Little valley and mountain folds are hidden.

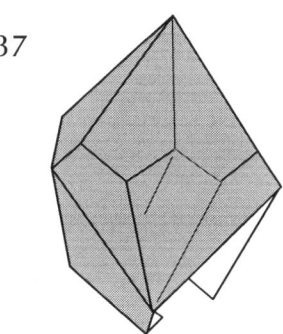

37

Repeat steps 32–35 two more times. The model closes with a three-way twist lock.

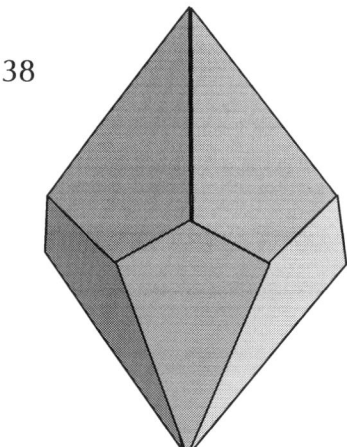

38

Hexagonal Trapezohedron

Golden Pentagonal Antiprism

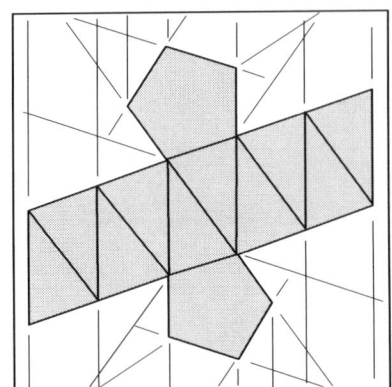

A pentagonal antiprism is composed of 10 triangles and two pentagons. In this one, the angles of each triangle are 36°, 72°, and 72°. The triangles form a band wrapping around.

1

Fold and unfold.

2

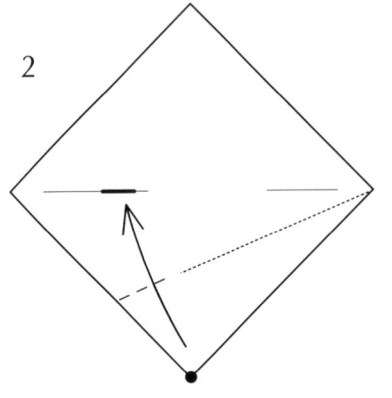

Crease on the left.

3

Unfold.

4

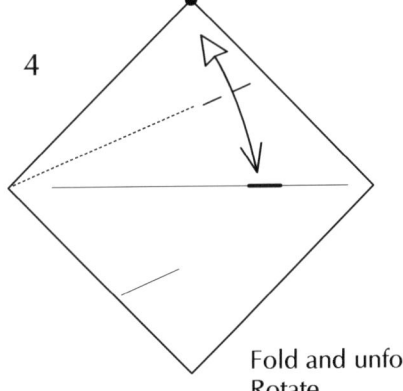

Fold and unfold. Rotate.

5

Fold and unfold.

6

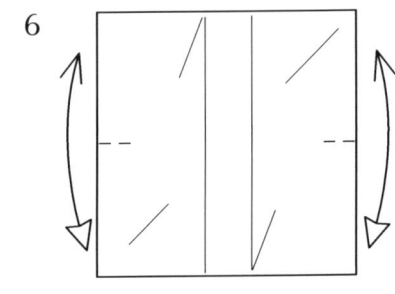

Fold and unfold in half at the edges.

108   *3D Origami Platonic Solids & More*

Golden Pentagonal Antiprism 109

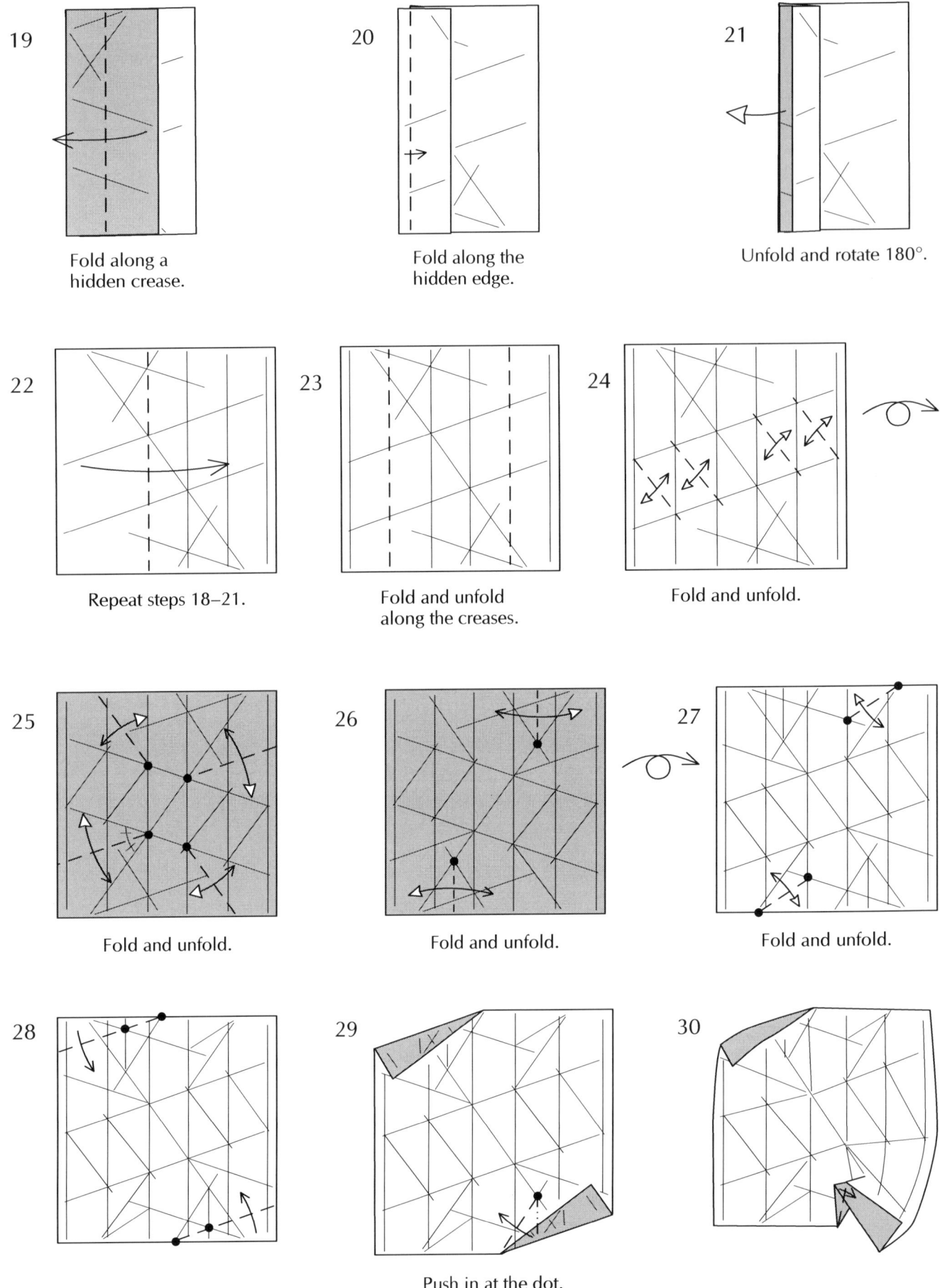

19. Fold along a hidden crease.

20. Fold along the hidden edge.

21. Unfold and rotate 180°.

22. Repeat steps 18–21.

23. Fold and unfold along the creases.

24. Fold and unfold.

25. Fold and unfold.

26. Fold and unfold.

27. Fold and unfold.

28.

29. Push in at the dot.

30.

31

Repeat steps 29–30 above. Rotate to view the outside so the dot is front and center.

32

Push in on the valley line. Fold along the creases. Turn over and repeat.

33

34

Tuck inside by wrapping around the layers.

35

Unfold to step 33.

36

Repeat steps 33–34.

37

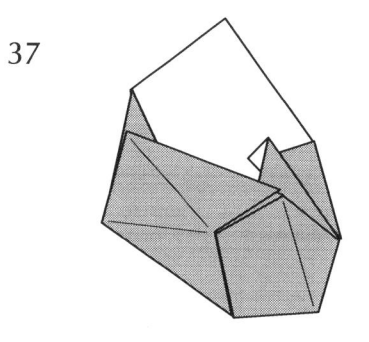

Refold steps 33–34 behind.

38

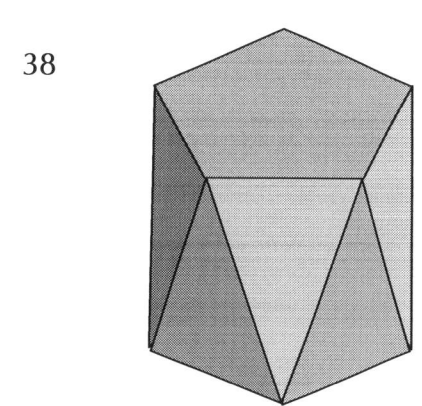

Golden Pentagonal Antiprism

Golden Pentagonal Antiprism 111

Triakis Tetrahedron

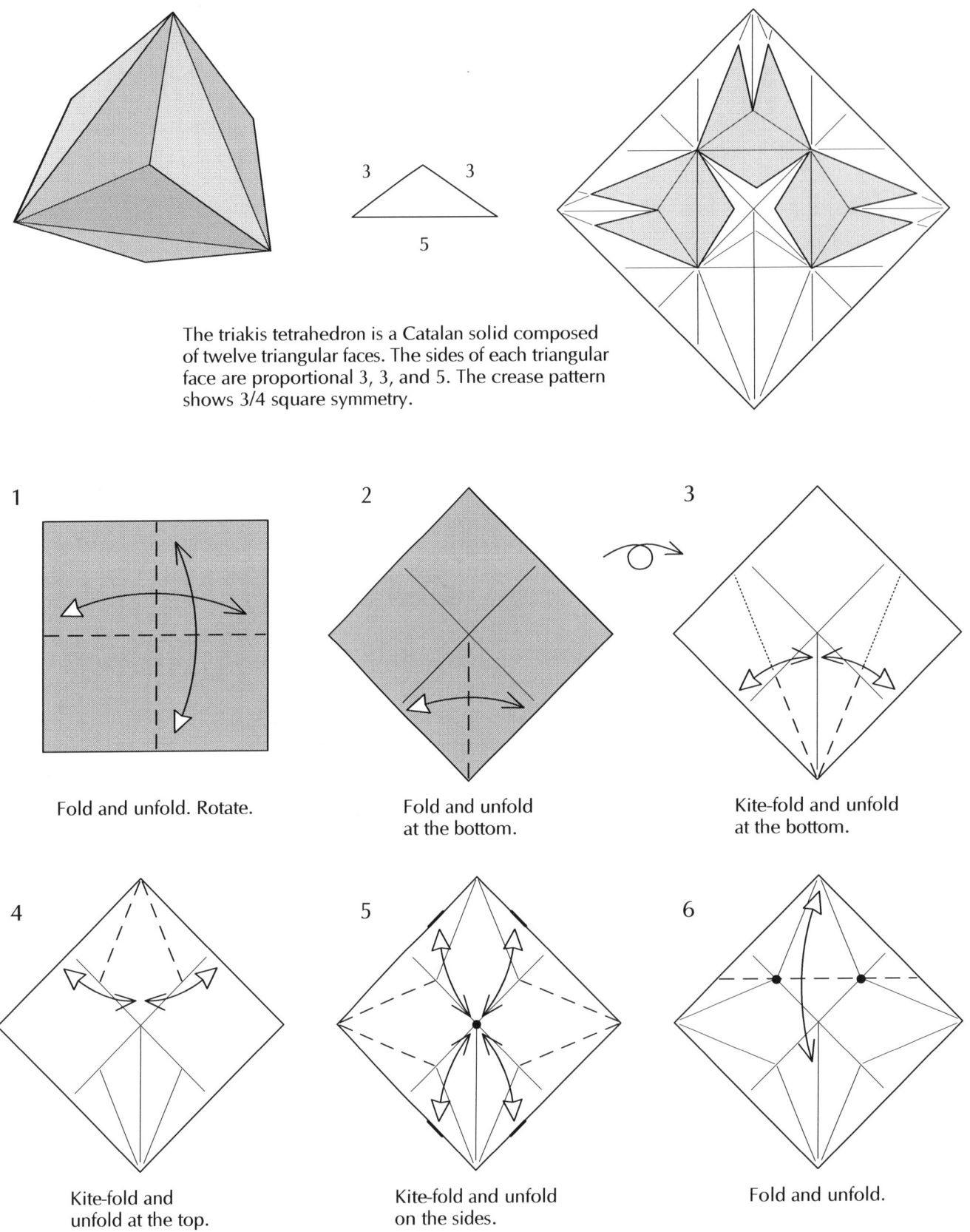

The triakis tetrahedron is a Catalan solid composed of twelve triangular faces. The sides of each triangular face are proportional 3, 3, and 5. The crease pattern shows 3/4 square symmetry.

1. Fold and unfold. Rotate.

2. Fold and unfold at the bottom.

3. Kite-fold and unfold at the bottom.

4. Kite-fold and unfold at the top.

5. Kite-fold and unfold on the sides.

6. Fold and unfold.

112   3D Origami Platonic Solids & More

7 Fold and unfold.

8 Fold and unfold. Rotate 90°.

9 Only crease on part of the line.

10 Unfold.

11 Only crease on part of the line.

12 Fold and unfold both layers along a hidden crease.

13 Unfold and rotate 90°.

14 Repeat steps 9–13 two more times.

15 Fold and unfold along the diagonals by three corners. Rotate.

17 Fold and unfold creasing lightly.

18 Fold and unfold.

Triakis Tetrahedron 113

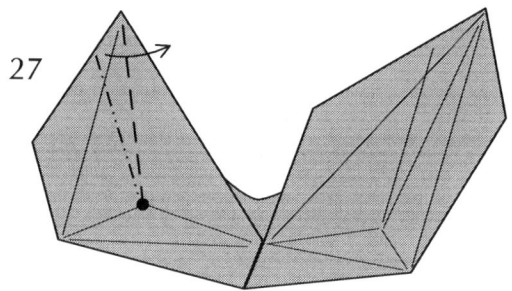

27. Puff out at the dot.

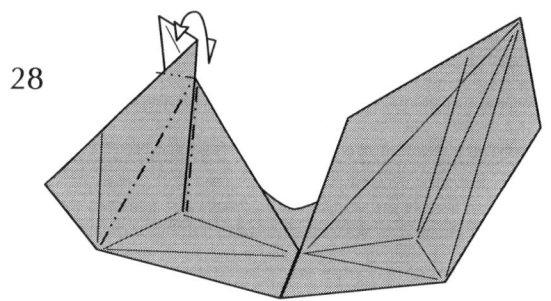

28. Fold and unfold at the top and along the crease and edge.

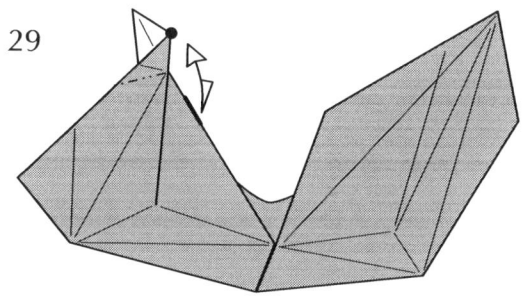

29. Fold and unfold. Rotate.

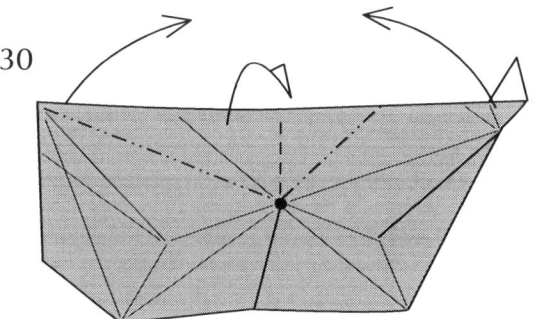

30. Repeat steps 26–29 two more times.

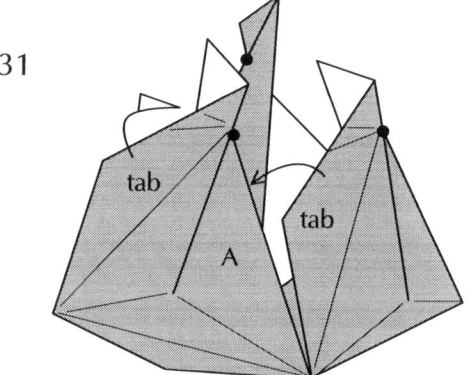

31. Tuck the tab behind region A. Continue all around. The three dots will meet. The model closes with a three-way twist lock.

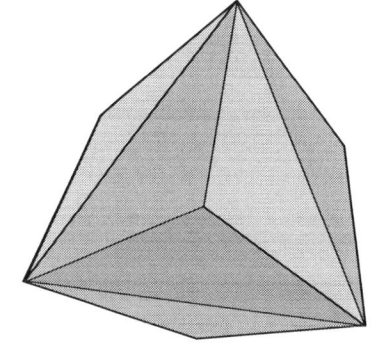

32.

Triakis Tetrahedron

Rhombic Dodecahedron

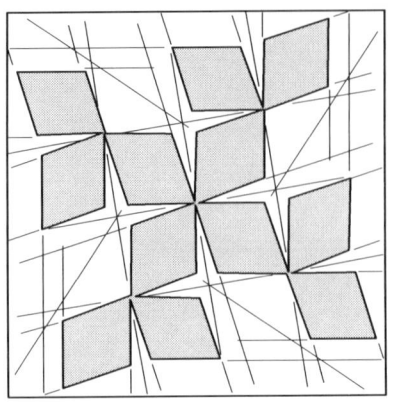

The rhombic dodecahedron is composed of twelve sides, each with diagonals proportional to 1 and $\sqrt{2}$. The model uses square symmetry and closes with a twist lock.

1

Fold and unfold.

2

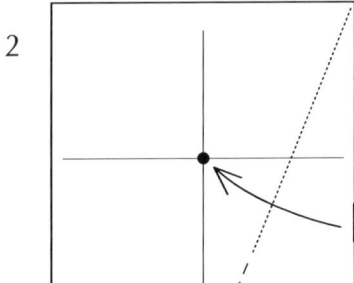

Bring the edge to the center and crease at the bottom.

3

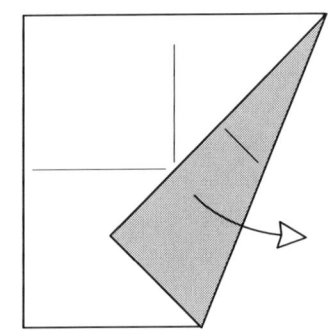

Unfold and rotate 180°.

4

Repeat steps 2–3.

5

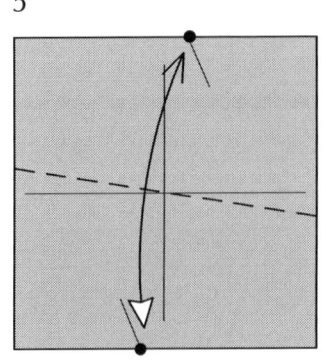

Fold and unfold.
Rotate 90°.

6

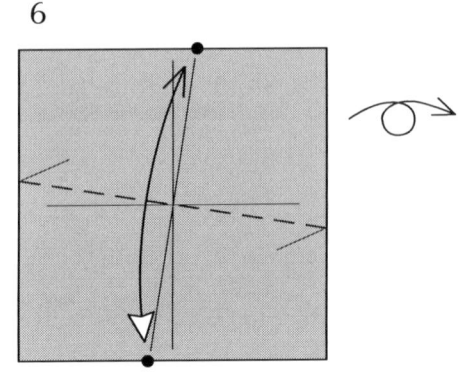

Fold and unfold.

116   *3D Origami Platonic Solids & More*

Rhombic Dodecahedron 117

30

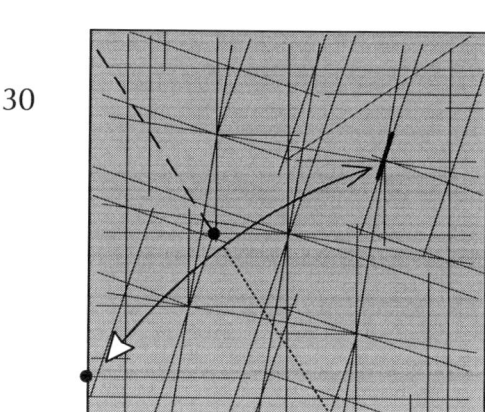

Repeat step 29 three more times.

31

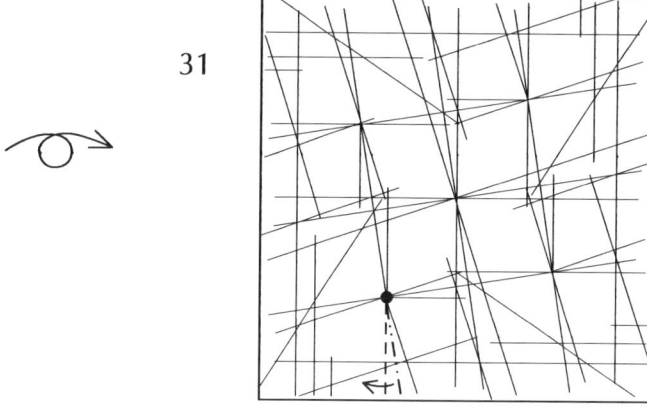

Fold along the creases and push in at the dot.

32

Valley-fold along the creases. Rotate 90°.

33

Repeat steps 31–32 three more times.

34

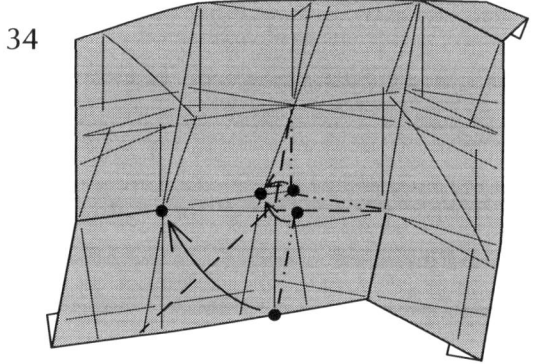

The groups of dots will meet.

35

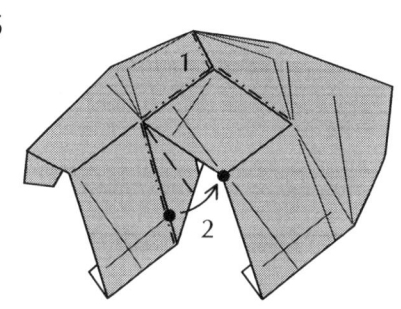

1. Fold and unfold along the edges.
2. The dots will meet.

Rhombic Dodecahedron 119

36
Unfold.

37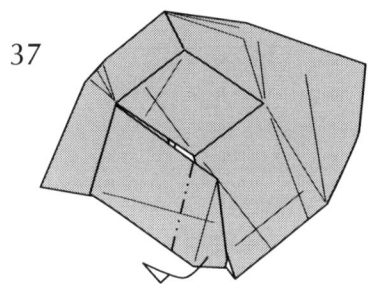
Fold along the crease.

38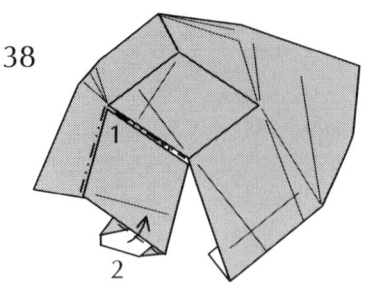
1. Fold and unfold along the edges.
2. Valley-fold.
Rotate 90°.

39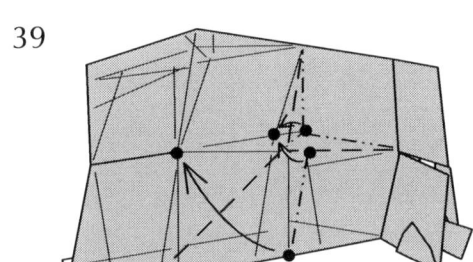
Repeat steps 34–38 three more times. Rotate the top to the bottom.

40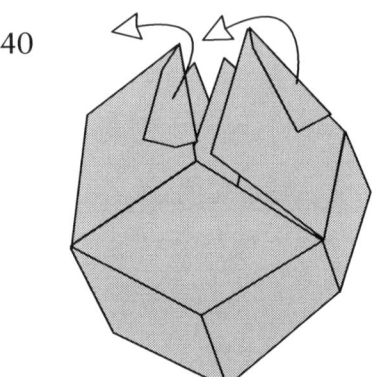
Unwrap the four tabs at the top.

41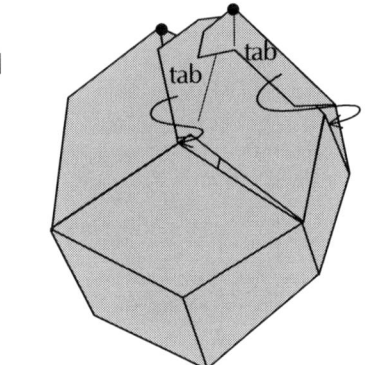
Tuck the four tabs inside to lock and close the model with a twist lock.

42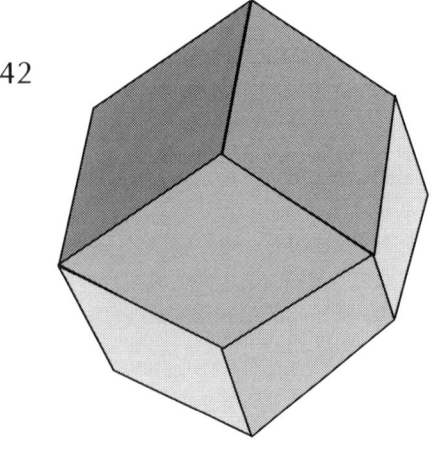

Rhombic Dodecahedron

120   *3D Origami Platonic Solids & More*

Made in the USA
Lexington, KY
13 May 2015